D0201122

Full Circle

Full Circle

AN AUTOBIOGRAPHY

Dan Jansen
with Jack McCallum

VILLARD BOOKS
NEW YORK • 1994

Library of Congress Cataloging-in-Publication Data
Jansen, Dan.
    Full circle: an autobiography / by Dan Jansen with Jack McCallum.
        p.   cm.
    ISBN 0-679-43801-7
    1. Jansen, Dan. 2. Skaters—United States—Biography. 3. Winter
Olympic Games (17th: 1994: Lillehammer, Norway) I. McCallum, Jack.
II. Title.
GV850.J36A3   1994
796.91'092—dc20   94-27211

First Edition

To my parents, Harry and Gerry

To Mary, Janet, Jim, Diane, Dick, Joanne, Jane, and Mike

To Robin and Jane

Without all of you, I would never have made it to the finish line

The authors thank the Jansen family members for their co-operation, as well as John Baskfield, Andy Gabel, Dr. Jim Loehr, Draggan Mihalovich, Pete Mueller, Rick Smith, and Nick Thometz.

Full Circle

CHAPTER 1

Lillehammer, Norway

● FEBRUARY 14, 1994

To most Americans, Winter Olympians are the hibernating animals of sport. Every few years or so we stick our noses out of our caves, venture into the cold to skate, ski, luge, or knock a hockey puck around, then disappear again, into the forest or to the North Pole or wherever it is we go until another Olympics rolls around again. Since Olympic sports are not the sports Americans follow from week to week (one of the all-time understatements), the Winter Olympic Games inevitably come down to a few easy-to-follow story lines, rather than what they should be—a hundred little mini-dramas, each with its own intrigue, tension, and heroes.

I guess I shouldn't complain, because I was clearly one of the story lines. It started in 1988 in Calgary, Canada, continued in 1992 in Albertville, France, and was certainly happening again on this day in Lillehammer, Norway. In no particular order, the major story lines of the 1994 Olympics were: Who will prevail in the Nancy Kerrigan–Tonya Harding soap opera? Will Bonnie Blair remain America's Winter Olympic sweetheart? Is the American alpine ski team really that bad? And will Dan Jansen screw up again?

Believe it or not, it was easier for someone in Lillehammer to avoid the Nancy-and-Tonya show than it was for someone back in the United States. I had arrived in Norway on February 1, before most of the athletes—my coach, Pete Mueller, thought it was important that I get acclimated early—and hadn't given figure skating more than a moment's thought. (For the record, I know Nancy fairly well and have rarely spoken to Tonya, so I guess my sentiments were for Kerrigan.) The speed skaters were somewhat isolated out in Hamar, a village about forty miles from the main Olympic village, and the television we watched was not the American networks (and certainly not *Hard Copy*) but rather Eurosport or satellite feeds. Eurosport ran a lot of replays from the world sprint championships that had taken place in late January in Calgary, so I got to lie around and watch myself winning both 500-meter races. It was great therapy.

My sports psychologist, Dr. Jim Loehr, also suggested that I stay away from the newspapers. That was fairly easy since most of them were in Norwegian. But I'm sure most of the English-language ones were devoting many, many column inches to the saga of Dan Jansen's Olympic moments, most of them bad.

I didn't like it, but I had to face it. Those closest to me—my wife, Robin, my family, my friends in the sport, the few observers and journalists who really understood speed skating—knew what I had accomplished over the last decade. I'm not bragging but merely stating a fact when I say that, regardless of my Olympic performances, I was destined to go down as one of the greatest speed skaters in history, maybe the greatest in the 500 meters. But to millions of other casual fans, I was either a choker, an Olympic klutz, or, at best, the all-time Heartbreak Kid. I was like that character in the *Li'l Abner* comic strip, Joe Btfsplk, who walked around with a rain cloud over his head. Only mine came with five Olympic rings. I hated those labels, but I couldn't deny their existence. My failures in Albertville two years earlier had become so linked with my two falls in Calgary in '88 that I bet half the Olympic audience wondered if I *ever* actually remained upright on a pair of skates.

Well, I did. Going into Lillehammer, I had dominated the 500 meters throughout that entire World Cup season and was probably the best 1,000-meter man, too. Pete Mueller, my coach, who never misses a chance to motivate, kept telling me that he had never seen anyone skate better for any extended period of time than I had in both events throughout the season. I wasn't going to argue with him. On the same ice where I was about to skate the Olympic 500, I had become the first person ever to go under 36 seconds in the 500 when I clocked 35.92 on December 4, 1993. To the people in our sport, it was comparable to Roger Bannister's four-minute mile, in that it was a psychological barrier to beat almost as much as it was a physiological one. A few weeks later I skated even faster in the world championships with a 35.76 on the same ice in Calgary where I had fallen in the '88 Olympics. It was the sixth time I had either set or tied the 500-meter world record.

But there were doubters, and I couldn't really blame them. When you compete in a sport where one one-hundredth of a second can separate first from second place and half a second is an eternity, anything can happen. (I had proven that conclusively in both '88 and '92.) Any little failure in form or momentary slip in precision can throw you off, and in that kind of sport nobody wins all the time. The 1993–94 season had been the best of my career, but still, three weeks before the Games, at a World Cup meet at the Pettit Center in Milwaukee ("home ice" for me), I had finished third in the 500 meters to two Japanese skaters, Yasunori Miyabe and Manabu Horii. After it was over they sounded like they were playing a few mind games. "I'll win the gold medal for Japan," Miyabe told the press. And Horii said, "I think I'll beat Jansen."

Mind games weren't something I paid a lot of attention to. My style on the ice has always been to take care of my own business and let everything else fall into place. Speed skating is not a sport for trash-talkers. But it's also true that as my career went on I started to pay more and more attention to the mental part of the sport. About nine months before the '92 Games in Albertville, my manager/agent at the time, Bennett Raffer, convinced me to visit a sports psychologist. I resisted the idea somewhat but finally relented because I knew I needed help. I desperately wanted to put the whole experience of the 1988 Olympics behind me, but I couldn't do it. In every single interview I did, in every single TV clip I saw, my falls in the 500 and the 1,000 and the death of my sister Jane were brought up.

"Dan, is there any way you can forget what happened in 1988?" I'd be asked.

"Well, yes, I think I can," I'd answer, "but only if everybody stops asking me about it." And everybody would laugh, and I'd laugh, and the next reporter would ask, "Dan, seriously, do you still think about falling?" "Do you still think about Jane?"

I treated the subject of my falling lightly, but obviously it was a heavy burden. The painful memory of February 14, 1988, the day Jane died and I fell in the 500 meters, combined with the flashbacks and images of falling in the 1,000, four days later, were a part of my everyday life, and more so when people asked me about them. Every athlete has to deal with his past failures, and I'm not suggesting that I should be any different. But the anonymity of our sport in the off-Olympic years virtually guarantees that Olympic experiences are *all* we have to deal with. That's not the case in other sports. For example, when Chris Webber called the timeout he didn't have, and maybe cost Michigan the NCAA championship in 1993, he had to deal with it. But fortunately for Chris, he's played a hundred games since then and has been able to show that his entire athletic career did not come down to one mistake made in the heat of battle. I didn't have that luxury.

Dr. Loehr (pronounced like "lair") helped me work through the burden of the '88 Olympics. And as I talked to him about the experience in Calgary and sorted out my feelings for perhaps the first time, we both began to see what had happened on the day Jane died. Two worlds had collided in my life: the world of what should've been the greatest day of my life, the Olympics, and the world of what was in fact the worst day of my life, the death of a sister to whom I had been extremely close. And something inside me simply would not *let* me experience the happiest day of my life on the saddest one. So I got out in front of everybody to show them that I could—that I *would*—deny myself triumph, that Jane's death was far more important than any Olympic medal, which was, of course, the absolute truth. And I proved that by falling down. Twice.

Does that mean I would've necessarily won two gold medals in 1988 if Jane had not died? Of course not. But the intense grieving that I went through, and my own inability to explain why I had fallen, particularly in the 1,000, a race I had dedicated to Jane, became clear to me for the first time and eased a giant mental burden. This happened late in 1991, after six months of work with Dr. Loehr, both in person and on the phone. What happened in Albertville a few months later, when I again didn't medal in either of my races? Well, that was a failure, too, and I'll talk about it later. But in my own mind I separate it completely from 1988. Finally being able to deal with Jane's death and the '88 Olympics was a huge mental breakthrough for me.

As I skated around Viking Ship Olympic Hall in Hamar a couple hours before my 1994 500-meter race, however, only those closest to me had any inkling of what was going on inside my head. My competitors saw a proficient skater at the top of his game, the guy everyone had to beat to win the gold, but I'm sure they also saw a man carrying around a ton of mental baggage, a man who would likely crack under pressure once again, a fragile psyche resting on top of a strong body.

They were wrong. By this stage in my life I was completely comfortable with who I was and the life I had chosen. Don't get me wrong—I don't think any of the 1,905 athletes at the Winter Games wanted a medal more than I did, and at the risk of sounding a bit self-serving I don't think any of them deserved a medal more than I did. Part of my mental motivation for Norway consisted of thinking that other people had something I truly thought should be in my own trophy case, i.e., an Olympic medal. But had I come away from Lillehammer empty-handed once again, my life would've gone on. No suicide, no bouts of depression, no turning to the bottle. Too many people—my wife, Robin, my daughter, Jane, my mom and dad, my three brothers and four sisters, Pete Mueller, Dr. Loehr, my longtime buddies in the sport like Andy Gabel, Nick Thometz, and of course Bonnie Blair—were around to give me love and support. And eventually the Olympic hurt would've gone away, and I would've been able to turn myself into something besides Dan Jansen, The Guy Who Never Won an Olympic Medal.

And there was another important element in my support system—the memory of my sister Jane. This day in Lillehammer was the sixth anniversary of her death, and my thoughts of her were still strong, as they were for my family. In our household, Valentine's Day was Jane's day. Too much time had passed to feel the pain as sharply as we used to, of course. The memory was more like an overall melancholy feeling that we did not resist, one that is simply a part of our lives. We're all sorry that she's gone, sorry that her three daughters will grow up without really knowing her. But it's also easy to remember the good times, too, because Jane was a very special person.

Jane

The worst thing about Jane dying when she did is that too many people will remember her only as a tragedy of the 1988 Olympics, or as the sister of Dan Jansen. I want her to be remembered as a person in her own right, someone with hopes and dreams, with faults and frailties, with special qualities.

Jane Jansen was the seventh of Harry and Geraldine Jansen's nine children. She was three and a half years older than Mike and five years older than me, the baby of the family. In such a large unit there are inevitably going to be "the older kids" and "the younger kids," and Jane, Mike, and I definitely made up the latter group. We were the tagalongs, the ones without all the responsibility. (Joanne, who was born two years before Jane, always complains that she was a "swing kid," too young to be an older kid, too old to be a younger kid.) Jane was easily the most sensitive Jansen, the one most attuned to other people's feelings and most vulnerable to criticism from the outside. I'm like Jane in a lot of respects (although I never cried as much, on the outside, as she did) in that I'm sensitive to the way people feel about me, though I try not to show it.

Naturally, Mike and I, being boys, were not above exploiting Jane's sensitivity. We'd make her cry, which was never hard to do, but she always forgave us. One of the legendary Jansen-kid stories, which my mother never tires of telling, was when Jane fell asleep on the couch and Mike and I put chocolate chips all over her to see if they would melt. They would. When Jane woke up she cried. When Mom got home she hollered, mostly, I think, because in a house with so many kids it was a crime to waste chocolate chips.

Jane was never cruel to anyone. Never. It was not in her nature. She was one of those people who was so nice, in fact, that you wondered if she was for real. Later, when she was dying, Diane, the fourth oldest, apologized to Jane for all the times she had hollered at her when they were kids. "Oh, Di, that didn't make any difference," Jane told her. "You were just being a mother to us." Four of my five sisters are nurses, but only Jane was too homesick to live at nursing school, which was only a few miles from home. And no matter how much we teased her, Jane was always ready to drive Mike and me wherever we wanted to go.

Jane was tough in her own way, though. When she was fourteen she developed scoliosis and had to wear a brace. She followed the doctor's orders religiously and only took that thing off for showers. She often slept on the couch because the brace was so uncomfortable and all she did was toss and turn. But she never complained.

All of my sisters are athletically inclined, but, next to Mary, the oldest, Jane was the best. She didn't have a lot of success in skating in the juniors because she was always going up against Mary Docter and Beth Heiden, who turned out to be two of America's best women skaters. But she was an excellent volleyball player and an outstanding softball pitcher. At one time, all five of my sisters played on the same softball team in our hometown of West Allis, Wisconsin, and they were practically unbeatable. Jane pitched, Janet played third base and the outfield, Mary played shortstop, Joanne was the catcher, and Diane played second. I went to a lot of their practices and even coached first base during the games. Being a small part of that team is one of my fondest memories.

Jane met her husband, Rich Beres, at a softball party.

They had three children. My oldest brother, Jim, always says that Jane wanted only two things out of life—to be a nurse and a mother—so, in that respect, she died satisfied. There's a lot of truth to that. But it would be ridiculous to call what happened to her anything but a tragedy.

On January 29, 1987, Jane gave birth to her third daughter, Jessica. Mary delivered Jessica, as she did several other of her nieces. Everything seemed normal. My parents got the word in Quebec, where they were watching me compete in a world sprint meet. When they returned they went directly from the airport to congratulate Jane and kiss their new granddaughter. There was some vaguely disturbing news, however. A routine blood test had discovered something, and Jane was asked to come back to the hospital. By that time I was home for a week before returning to Europe for the remainder of the World Cup season. On the morning of February 4, Jane got the news—she had leukemia.

I remember coming home that morning after working out, and, for reasons I can't remember, Bonnie Blair was with me. Probably she was just stopping over to say hello to the family, whom she had known for some time. I knew that Jane had gone in for tests, but I hadn't really paid it much mind since she was such a healthy, athletic person. She had played a game of volleyball the night before she gave birth, after all. Dad and my oldest brother, Jim, were in the living room, and right away I knew something was wrong when I saw Dad with red eyes.

"They've diagnosed Jane with leukemia," said Jim, the member of the family least likely to mince words.

I knew it was real serious, of course, and I knew basically that the disease was a horrible one. But my mind fought against it and my first reaction was "Okay, well, how do we fix that? What do we do now?"

Jim just shook his head and said, "You usually die from leukemia."

I remember my heart sank. Just sank. I gave my father a hug, went back to my bedroom with Bonnie, and started crying. Why? Why Jane? Why us? To that point in my life I hadn't known real tragedy. Sadness was a bad workout, tragedy was finishing out of the medal count in a World Cup race. I leaned on Bonnie a lot over those next couple hours. I'm glad she was there. The plan was for the whole family to meet at Jane's later in the day to discuss the situation, and I remember going back to the rink wearing a pair of sunglasses to keep anyone from seeing my eyes.

Maybe it'll go away, I thought as I drove to Jane's. Maybe it's all a bad dream. Maybe the tests are wrong. But when I entered the house and saw all my brothers and sisters and in-laws, and then I saw Jane, I knew it was true. We held each other for a long time. Later I found out what Jane's first reaction had been. "Oh, my God, Rich," she said to her husband. "I'm going to die and you'll have to take care of the kids alone." Besides Jessica, her other daughters, Susie and Amy, were only three and one and a half years old.

Nobody was ready to give up, of course. My mother had already dug out the textbooks and was doing her research. And I honestly believe that right up until the end, which was a little more than a year from that awful day, Jane believed she could beat it. Then, too, we were all deeply religious people, not the kind who preached about miracles on street corners, but people with a deep and abiding belief in God. However, a sense of reality pervaded the family. My mother and four of my sisters, including Jane, were nurses; Mary was working at the hospital where Jane had been tested and had seen the worried looks that passed between the doctors when they got the results. My father was a policeman, and so were two of his sons and one of his daughters. And Jane's husband, Rich, was a fireman. People in those kinds of jobs deal with reality every single day of their lives. Nobody spoke openly about it, not in the beginning anyway, but we all knew that Jane's fight was going to be long, hard, and, in the end, probably futile.

One of the first things to be done with a leukemia patient is to find a match for a bone marrow transplant. As luck would have it, both Joanne and I were perfect. I was in Europe for a World Cup meet by the time the match was discovered and immediately wrote Jane a letter telling her that I'd be more than willing to be the donor. Later, that got a lot of attention, as if I deserved credit for it. That's absurd. Any member of our family would've done the same thing, no matter what the consequences. They quickly decided on Joanne to be the donor for three reasons: first, I had been sick with mononucleosis not long before that; second, women usually make healthier donors than men; third, there was consideration given to my skating career. The decision to use Joanne made a lot of sense, even though I meant every word of what I told Jane in the letter.

In that letter I also remember apologizing for all the

problems I had unloaded on her over the years. Being away from family so much of the time in Europe and facing the constant pressure of competition can be hard on the mind, and Jane was the one I leaned on. My problems were never insurmountable ones, and the death of a loved one makes you realize that fact even more. But you're not thinking about anything but yourself when you're feeling down and alone and eating strange food in a boardinghouse where no one speaks English. In retrospect, I suppose that was the most unusual thing about the bond between Jane and me. I could always talk to her, and I think that's rare for brother and sister. But that's just the way Jane was.

From February 1987 until her death on February 14, 1988, Jane's struggle was one of peaks and valleys. But she never outwardly wavered from the belief that she would beat the disease. Her courage was unbelievable, and she was even able to have a sense of humor about her condition. One time a doctor who had invented a particular kind of cancer treatment was administering it to her, and Jane looked at him and said, "Say, have you done this before?"

I was away much of the time competing and training

for the '88 Olympics in Calgary. Jane spent a lot of time out in a cancer hospital in Seattle where the transplant was to be done, and at one point I visited her and donated platelets, which she needed for her treatment. She was supposed to stay only a few weeks, but all kinds of problems arose and they had to wait much longer than expected to do the transplant. In fact, her doctors even told her she could go back home and return for the operation.

"No, I'll stay," Jane decided. "I told my little girls that Mommy will be back when she's healthy, and if I go back now they'll think I'm okay." So she stayed in Seattle. It must've been a desperately hard time for her husband and also for my mom and dad, who stayed out there with her. Jane finally had the transplant in September 1987 and came home in early October. I remember going over to see her before I had to leave again for fall training in Europe. The radiation treatments had left her bald, but she looked beautiful. We stood outside in her yard for a long time, by the road, hugging and talking, laughing and crying, and something came back to me. A couple years earlier, a few of the Jansens had been down at the Happy Tap, a bar in West Allis. The subject of the world championships had come up, and Jane had said, "Well, when Dan wins the worlds . . ." Not "if." *When.* The faith Jane had in me meant a lot.

As I got ready to leave that day, Jane's good-bye was typical. "Now, don't worry about me. I'll be fine. Put this out of your mind and concentrate on your skating." Though I didn't know it at the time, it was to be the last extended conversation we ever had.

I returned home to West Allis for the Olympic trials in December. The bone marrow transplant seemed to work at first, and Jane had some healthy weeks in the fall. Then, suddenly, things got worse. On December 11, just after I finished my first 500 and was putting on my guards, there was Dad, red-eyed again, standing over me.

"Jane's out of remission," he said. She went back into West Allis Memorial and, except for one brief home visit one afternoon, never left the hospital again.

If God wanted to test the Jansen family that year, He succeeded. Mom and Dad felt bad because they had been watching me in the trials instead of being with Jane. I felt bad because I was concentrating on something so frivolous as skating around an oval while my sister was dying. And Jane felt bad because she was causing everybody so much trouble. That's just the way she was. It was the worst kind of timing. And the problem I later had in dealing with my feelings of guilt could be traced to those days. How could I worry about making the Olympic team when my sister was worrying about staying alive? Shouldn't I chuck it all and stay by her side at the hospital? Yet skating was a major part of my life and, moreover, a part of my life that Jane did not want to disturb. Somehow, I skated well enough to earn a spot on both the 500- and 1,000-meter teams, but my mind was far from the ice.

As luck would have it, the world sprint championships were held back home in early February 1988, one week before the Calgary Olympics, and I skated well enough to win my first world title. Not if. *When.* There was no chance that Jane could make it to the rink, but I went directly to the hospital with my medal and held it up to her eyes. She couldn't have been happier if she had won it herself. We hugged and laughed and cried, and it was at that moment that I really became aware of the importance of my family members, how their collective strength had helped me accomplish so much.

I said good-bye to Jane. She wished me luck in Calgary. I never saw her alive after that.

In the few interviews she did while she was sick, Jane was of course asked the inevitable question: Did you ask Dan to win a gold medal for you? Jane was genuinely disturbed by this. "I would never do something like that," she said. "That would put far too much pressure on him. And the only thing I want is what everybody in our family wants, which is for him to do the best he can do."

Well, Jane, I did win one for you. It just took a little bit longer than I thought it would.

CHAPTER 2

Lillehammer

As I warmed up before my 500-meter race two hours hence, I thought about how much I truly loved this sport. Considering what I've gone through, I guess it's a good thing, right? I never wavered in my love for skating, even in the bad moments after 1988 and '92, and never regretted the decision I made to dedicate myself to it way back when I was sixteen years old.

What was it in my personality that made me a speed skater? There were so many things, really. I've never been afraid of hard work, for one thing. I'm not a masochist, but I am willing to pay the price, which comes in hours of long, lonely drudgery. And "drudgery" is the operative word. To get a true picture of the sport's "glamour," everyone should sit down and watch a home videotape that my family made for me a long time ago. In one of the small upstairs bedrooms of my parents' house, Andy Gabel and I are taking turns on a "slide board," a three-by-seven-foot hunk of white Formica with blocks of wood at each end. We're sliding back and forth, back and forth, staring into a mirror to hold our skating position, back low, left arm tucked behind, a pair of ratty, oversized socks on our feet, filling that small room with our sweat, an exercise so monotonous it makes the stationary bike look like a roller-coaster ride. Whenever my brother Mike and I want to remember the good old days of skating, all we have to do is mention "Sunday morning" and "Olympia ski hill." As the highlight of that day's workout, we'd duckwalk all the way up that darn hill, come down, then do it again. If you didn't throw up once or twice, we used to say, you didn't feel fulfilled. You think we didn't come to dread Sundays? But up that hill we went, looking like some kind of bad imitation of Groucho Marx. And what you have to remember about these workouts is that for the vast majority of the time there is no coach around to push you, no whistles, no buzzers, no team huddles. Under those circumstances, your own work ethic comes out, and it had better be a strong one.

Though I do a pretty good job of disguising it, I'm highly competitive, too. I've always been that way. One of my oldest friends, Rick Smith, who's now a lawyer in Milwaukee, remembers me hollering at him once in a while during Little League games, but gradually I was able to hide my competitiveness better. Robin jokes that even when we're stacking dishes, I have a need to get them into the dishwasher faster than she does. But I don't know of a world-class athlete who isn't competitive, not one who's stayed at the top for a long time, anyway.

Then, too, there must be something inside me that values precision. Though I enjoyed football and baseball, I seemed to like beating a clock even more than I liked beating opponents. I relished the challenge of making subtle adjustments that cut a couple hundredths off my time. Speed skating is not a sport for the impatient athlete, to say the least. It's a sport where you control your own destiny, where there are no teammates to pull you along or drag you down, and that appealed to me, too.

At 6'0" and 195 pounds, I'm a little bigger than the average sprinter, but certainly not too big. Some people are surprised to find that the sprinters, the 500- and 1,000-meter guys, are actually bigger and stronger than the endurance skaters, the 5,000- and 10,000-meter guys. But it's understandable and comparable to the differences between the heavily muscled track sprinters and the no-body-fat, skinny distance runners. The bigger the thighs, the more the buildup of lactic acid, which is what causes fatigue. The sprinters, guys like me, want the race to be over before the lactic acid takes its toll.

It would also be silly of me to deny the importance of natural talent in the sport. Pete Mueller says that he can take a skater of average talent and physical skills and turn him into an acceptable endurance skater, but there is no way he could turn someone with limited natural ability into a world-class sprinter. Your ability to get off the line is just too important. I always had that, not necessarily more than anyone else, but certainly just as much. I'm a better-than-average sprinter on the track— and I was a pretty good running back in football. Those skills are not entirely transferable to skating, but they're not irrelevant either.

But it wasn't until I really began working with Dr. Loehr that I realized the necessity of uniting the mind and the body. As I said, I wasn't a believer at first and went to him only because I was desperate to obliterate the painful memories of 1988. When I went to his office in Florida, I made sure I took one of my skating buddies, Nick Thometz, with me. But it's no coincidence that I had my greatest season, 1993–94, as both a skater and a human being, after I started to live and truly believe in Dr. Loehr's program.

One of the most helpful things he did was help me design a "mental war room" for myself, a place to which I could escape before my races. He told me to equip it with everything that made me feel good. I had pictures of Robin and baby Jane, pictures of my family, trophies from races that had special meaning for me, special music and tapes I liked, Garth Brooks and Jimmy Buffett to name two. (I would've put an Olympic medal in there, but I didn't have one.) As I came off the ice and sat down in the locker room about ninety minutes before my 500-meter race, I paid a quiet visit to my war room.

Dr. Loehr ignored nothing, overlooked nothing. Over time he became conversant with speed skating (he's now something of an expert on lap times and the like), but most of his principles are general ones that can be applied to any sport. My sleep habits, my stress level, my inner-directed feelings, my meals, all those things had to do with what I was as a person and as an athlete. I was religious in writing it all down and faxing it to him from wherever I was on the road. Here's a sample from a particularly important week in late November and early December, the week I broke that 36-second barrier on the very ice where my 500-meter Olympic race was to take place:

DAILY STRESS & DIARY FOR
DAN JANSEN

Physical Stress (Training)	1 Low	2	3	4	(5)	6	7	8	9	10 High
Emotional Stress (Training)	1 Low	2	3	4	(5)	6	7	8	9	10 High
Emotional Stress (Life)	1 Low	(2)	3	4	5	6	7	8	9	10 High
Overall Stress	1 Low	2	(3)	4	5	6	7	8	9	10 High
Overall Recovery	1 Low	2	3	4	5	6	7	(8)	9	10 High
Feel Good About Me	1 No	2	3	4	5	6	7	8	9	(10 Yes)
Express Feelings	1 No	2	3	4	5	6	7	8	9	(10 Yes)

DAILY DIARY

World Cup - Hamar, Norway
1st 500 - 35.92!! I did it! 1st person ever under 36! 1st place
2nd 500 - 35.96 Did it again! With a last inner turn! Even with 1 slip! Remember this feeling!
1000 - 1:13.01 1st Place
Very good race, Great weekend! Keep it up!

FRAME

Very Relaxed + Confident now!

DAILY MONITORING CHART

FOR DAN JANSEN

	Travel					Race	Race
	Mon	Tues	Wed	Thurs	Fri	Sat	Sun
Interval Exercise (Time)	—	30'	—	—	—	—	—
Aerobic Exercise (Time)	—	45'	sprints	60'	easy	500	500/1500
Strength Training (Time)	—	plyos	—	—	—	—	—
Diet (A–F)	B	A –	A –	B	B	B	B
Number of Meals	3	3	3	3	3	3	3
Sugar # of Times	3	2	2	2	3	2	2
Quantity of R & R (Time)	2hrs	4hrs	4hrs	4hrs	6hrs	3hrs	3hrs
Quality of R & R (A–F)	B	B+	A –	B	B+	B	B
Time to Bed/Time Up	10:30/8:00	11:00/8:00	11:00/8:50	11:00/8:00	11:00/7:00	11:00/8:00	11:00
Hours of Sleep	9	9	9½	10	4	7½	
Quality of Sleep (A–F)	A	A	A	A	F	B	
Nap (Yes/No)	No	Yes	Yes	Yes	Yes	Yes	No
Positive Attitude (A–F)	A	A	A	A	A	A	A
Confident Fighter Image (A–F)	—	A	A	A	A	A+	A+
Concentration Today (A–F)	—	A	A	A	A	A	A
Confidence Today (Yes/No)	Yes	Yes	Yes	Yes	Yes	Yes	Yes
Motivation Today (A–F)	—	A	A	A-	A-	A	A
Had Fun Today (A–F)	—	A	A	A-	A	A+	A+
Relaxation Exercise (Time)	—	—	—	—	—	—	—
Feel Energy (A–F)	—	B+	A	A	A	A	A
How Well I Performed (A–F)	—	A	A	A	A+	A+	A+

The idea is not to build a perfect athlete or a perfect human being, because that won't happen. You'll notice that there's an F in the middle of all those A's in my "quality of sleep" category, which came the night before I broke the 500-meter record. But what Dr. Loehr is striving for is balance, balance between your sport and your life. If you train this much, you need that much time to recover. The monitoring sheets were a way of making sure I was doing the right things all the time. I had always kept a journal of my workouts but it was downright simplistic compared to this high-level record keeping. I came to enjoy the process because it seemed to relax me and keep me motivated.

As Dr. Loehr himself gradually realized, though, perhaps the most important ingredient that went into making me a champion was one that I had no control over and deserved no credit for. That was my support system, which was extraordinary in both its size and resilience. And as my 500-meter race crept closer and closer, I conjured up my positive feelings about the people around me and truly believed that no athlete in Lillehammer could call on family and friends to the extent that I could. Was I able to precisely quantify the importance of that to my skating? Of course not. But so much of what I was, what I believed, and what I was trying to achieve began with the steadfast, loving people who stood behind me.

Beginnings

Nothing confuses my parents more than when someone asks them, "So, what's your secret?" They simply don't have an answer. They don't know how they raised nine children on a policeman's salary and a part-time nurse's salary. They don't know why the kids all stick together and still love each other like some Wisconsin version of *The Waltons.* They don't know how all the kids stayed out of trouble, avoided scandal and embarrassment. They just don't know.

The Jansen kids can't answer it, either. But all eight of us know—just as Jane knew when she was alive— that the example of our parents held this family together. They didn't have a lot of rules and regulations or a lot of guidelines to follow. They simply pointed the way by example and we all followed. And to know me and my story, you should know something about my parents.

My mother, Geraldine (who would rather be called Gerry), was brought up on the south side of Milwaukee, the daughter of an Irish mother and a Polish father whose last name was Grajek. The neighborhood was highly ethnic—the grandmother on her father's side, her "buscha," spoke only Polish until the day she died—but my mom's mother demanded that her children speak the king's English. If she or any of her four brothers and sisters spoke a word that did not meet her mother's standards—like making "this" and "that" sound like "dis" and "dat"—they were grounded. My mother was never that strict about anything, but, if either of my parents could be described as the enforcer, she was the one. She was also the holder of the purse strings. If you want to set my mom off, just mention that you think it's a good idea when high school kids toilet-paper trees as a show of school spirit. She'll give you a nice lecture about waste.

My mom went to nursing school in Milwaukee, and it was there she first laid eyes on Harry Jansen, one of five Jansen boys who grew up in a house only a few blocks from what is now the Pettit Center. My mom says they met at a dance called a "turnaround," which sounds like a skating maneuver but was in fact a night when the girls asked the boys out. My dad's father, who made a solid living managing a large warehouse in Milwaukee, was a big man who played lineman on a town football team that once played against the old Green Bay Packers. Most of his sons were big, too, including my father, who at Nathan Hale High School in West Allis played linebacker and tackle in football and center in basketball. (My mother complains, gently, that when television shows the Jansen family in the stands, Harry is so big that nobody sees her.) He was all-conference and honorable mention all-state in both sports. The funny thing is, he never skated much, even though there was an active skating community in West Allis and his ancestral roots lie in Holland and Belgium. He was just too busy doing other things, and my mother always remembers him saying, "Skating will hurt my basketball because it's so tough on your ankles."

My father and his brother Jim, who was two years older, wanted to play college football together. They were very, very close, just like Mike and I were when we skated together. They started at Northwestern, transferred together to Southern Cal, and came back to Marquette. College never quite worked out for my dad, and he eventually quit and got a job on the West Allis police force. He made detective after nine years, then detective sergeant, and finally lieutenant of detectives. From time to time he has a few regrets about not graduating from college, and he always took an interest in the college achievements of my friends who did go, like Andy Gabel. But Dad is proud of what he accomplished, as he should be, and says that one of the best things about his life was that he never dreaded going to work.

Mom and Dad got married in 1950 and have been in West Allis ever since. They've lived in the same house for thirty-three years, the one I was born and raised in. Coming from large families did not scare them off, and they wanted one of their own. Whether or not they intended to produce an entire starting baseball team, I don't know. Now is as good a time as any to introduce the Jansen children. There's extra credit if you keep us all straight.

Mary was the first. Fifteen months later came Janet. Eighteen months later came Jim. One year later came Diane. Fifteen months later came Dick. Eighteen months later came Joanne. Two years and nine months later came Jane. Two years later came Mike. And eighteen months later came Dan. The only one disappointed with Dan was Diane. Diane had reached the age where she was allowed to name the final baby if it was a girl, and she intended to have a Christine Jansen in the family. Sorry, Diane.

Whenever Mom wants to talk about the kids, she has to begin at the top and work her way down to keep them all straight. She can't just leap in to talk about, say, Jim without first mentioning Mary and Janet. And even though I came back from Lillehammer with a gold medal, I'm still at the bottom of the speed-dialing pecking order at my parents' house. Mary, the oldest, is number two (number one doesn't work), and I'm number nine.

The Jansen kids' personalities are similar, a combination of my mom's and my dad's. Jim is a little more aggressive and action-oriented than the rest of us; he's with the New Berlin police department, and every year he's the guy busting everyone's butt to get out and practice for the full-contact football game against the fire department. And Diane is the outspoken one; when I plugged my new boom box into the wrong outlet in East Germany and blew it up a few years ago, Diane's the one who took it back to the store and got a new one at no cost. Neither of my parents, or me for that matter, could've done that. But except for a few differences like that, anyone would recognize us all as Jansens.

There's no doubt we got our athletic ability from our father, who was a natural at everything he tried. He was such a good athlete that one of my sisters remembers meeting a woman who used to date him a long time ago; the woman was married by this time, and her husband spoke up and said, "Just think, honey, if you had married Harry Jansen instead of me, *your* son would've been an Olympic athlete." As if my mother had nothing to do with it. Actually, she never tried organized sports much, but she was a pretty good swimmer. My father was one of those athletes who was also a gifted teacher. He taught Diane the right way to sweep the kitchen floor the same way he taught Mary and Janet how not to throw like girls. And he did it all with patience.

We were not exactly a scandalous family. We had our moments, just not many of them. One time Jim started a fight in the park and came home minus a couple teeth. The sisters invented an elaborate story about Jim's assailant, and the police were called in to find the perpetrator. When they asked questions the next day, someone at the park said, "Oh, yeah, Jim Jansen started that fight." The jig was up.

When Dick was in high school, he and a couple of friends broke a Halloween jack-o'-lantern on a neighbor's lawn, then jumped into a getaway car that wouldn't start. My father found out and sent Dick back to clean it up. Janet once stayed away from school on senior skip day, but even then she went to a phone booth, called the school, and pretended to be my mother saying she was sick. As I said, the Jansens were *not quite* synonymous with scandal.

It is at once easy and hard to explain why we stayed in line. My father. Harry Jansen never raised his voice and never even threatened to hit us, but we just didn't want to screw up as long as he was around. And it wasn't fear of him that kept us in line but, rather, respect. Janet literally gets tears in her eyes when she tells the story of Jim's fight at the park because she still feels bad that she lied to my father. For that reason I never even heard that story until I was twenty years old. It was the same way with my friends. One time Rick Smith and I were playing by the railroad tracks, where we shouldn't have been, and I fell and cut my wrist and ripped my clothes. "Man, you're gonna get it," Rick said. And he was just amazed when all my father did was look at me and say, "Oh, boy." That's when you knew you were in trouble with my father. "Oh, boy." Andy Gabel used to joke around with me and say, "How many 'oh, boy's did you get today?" I hope someday I can keep my kids on the straight and narrow with the "oh, boy" school of discipline, but I expect it will be difficult.

But he and my mother worked together, too. They never contradicted each other and always kept a united front when one of the kids had to be disciplined. One of my mom's rules was that if someone invited one Jansen kid, they all had to be able to go. If a neighbor wanted Joanne and not Jane, Joanne didn't go, either. I'm sure some of the older ones got sick of the younger ones from time to time (I never had anybody to get sick of), but it did develop a feeling of closeness among the family. I think we all feel that if we can give our kids what our parents gave us, we will have been successful parents.

One of the highest compliments I can pay my parents is that they made a comfortable home not just for us, but for anyone who crossed our doorstep. After I started skating, there was rarely a time when someone wasn't staying at my house during meets and training. Andy Gabel even spent several months there earlier this year while his new condo was being built, and he used the same house key he had when he was a student at Marquette. He swears my mother had tears in her eyes when he left for his new condo. That kind of feeling rubbed off. Every single one of us still lives in or around West Allis, which is extraordinary when you think about it. Jim's house is eleven miles away from my parents', which makes him practically an alien. Diane jokes that she'll never forgive him because she needed a map to find his house the first time, and she tells me that I'm not allowed to live more than four miles from Mom and Dad. Right now, Robin, Janie, and I live about three miles away. I sometimes wonder if it's strange for Robin, a southern girl, to have been dropped into the middle of a dozen Jansens in Wisconsin, but she likes living where we do as much as I do.

Subconsciously, I suppose that living near my parents is an attempt to replicate some of the experiences I had growing up, even though it probably won't happen. Robin and I simply won't have to make the sacrifices that my parents made for me. Times are different, and I know we won't be having a nine-kid family. But I am absolutely convinced that growing up in a large, extended family the way I did is a gift. Our family has had its problems and arguments, just like everyone else, but none of us has ever lost sight of the fact that family is the most important thing in our lives. We like being around one another, we respect one another, we look out for one another, we love one another. That's our simple definition of what a family does.

—

Maybe I never would've started skating if Mary, the oldest, hadn't been prone to sickness in the winter months. Mary was a terrific athlete but didn't have many opportunities to participate in sports once it got cold, so she tended to lie around the house and cough a lot. My father thought it was because she was inside all the time. So one Sunday morning he decided to take her over to McCarty Park, which is only a quarter mile from our house, to watch the North American Skating Championships. Mary was about ten years old and had never had a pair of skates on her feet. As she watched the competitors, she turned to my dad and said, "I can do that."

And that's how the Jansen family started skating.

It was fortunate that Mary went out that day, but it wasn't necessarily preordained. Had she not started and been successful, maybe I would've paid more attention to football and baseball. Who knows? It's entirely possible. But once it happened, West Allis was an ideal place to develop as a speed skater, maybe *the* best place in the country. The West Allis Speed Skating Club was born during the Depression in the 1930s and is still going strong today. In most other Wisconsin towns boys start playing hockey automatically, but in West Allis they begin speed-skating. The tradition was there. As early as 1936 a guy named Del Lamb from the club made the Olympics, and in 1956 William Carow did it with Lamb as his coach. One of the most famous West Allis guys to make the Olympics was Wayne LeBombard, in 1964 and '68. And then came a few guys I knew—Mike Woods and Tom and Mike Plant.

Mary had a knack for skating right away and became a state champion. The skating back then, the kind we all started in, was pack-style, the kind you see in Olympic short-track skating. Janet used to go watch Mary from the warming house, and gradually she took it up, and then so did Diane. Janet became a state champ, too, and was actually the first Jansen to skate the 500 meters on an official oval. She went under 48 seconds the first time she tried it, and my mother remembers that everyone was talking about it. (As a basis for comparison, Bonnie

Blair now skates it under 40 seconds.) But none of my sisters had any professional training, and, had they been born later, in an era when girls were "supposed" to be athletes, I think they could've gone far, maybe even been world-class. But for them it was largely a social event. Jane always said that her favorite memory of youth skating was watching Eric Heiden, who was from Madison but who used to come over and skate in West Allis, take off his pants to change into his skating tights right in the middle of the rink. That activity was eventually banned. Janet remembers being shocked one day when Mrs. LeBombard, who was involved in youth skating, said to her, "With the right training, we're gonna have two inches on those thighs by the end of the summer." That is not what Janet wanted to hear.

Our parents never, ever pushed us into skating. That's important to remember. Diane tried it, had some success, but didn't really pursue it. That was fine. Joanne tried it, wasn't very successful at all, and asked Dad if she could quit. He was genuinely perplexed by the question. "Why would you do something you don't like?" he said. So Joanne hung up the skates.

After Mary and Janet set the pace, my brothers just naturally followed. Jim was an above-average skater but could never beat the real good guys who were around then, one of them being Pete Mueller, who later became my coach. Dick, however, was really good, and in many ways he's the most remarkable skater of any of us. I wasn't born when this happened, but my father remembers Dick at a meet when he was about five years old wearing a pair of white girls' figure skates laced up around his ankles. He took off in this race, but they fired the gun a second time to indicate a restart. Dick either didn't hear the gun or didn't care. He kept on going all the way around the track, never noticing that everyone else was back at the starting line. When he finished, he just wouldn't believe that he hadn't won the race, and he refused to go back to the line. There's a stubborn kid.

Dick won several state championships and finished third in the nationals as a junior but concentrated on other sports in high school, like football, swimming, and track. He decided to get back into skating a few years ago, and since then he's won consecutive national championships in the masters' division, which is for skaters thirty-five to fifty years of age. He also had a goal of trying to qualify for the Olympic trials in 1992, which took an unbelievable commitment on his part.

He's a sergeant in the West Allis police department and works the midnight–to–8 A.M. shift. He'd change into his skating clothes at work, go directly to a workout, come home, shower, grab something to eat, lie down for a couple hours, do an afternoon workout, then go directly to work again. Unbelievable.

The cutoff time to make the trials was 40.5 seconds for the 500 meters, and Dick made it on his last attempt. (I'm not the only Jansen with a sense of drama.) So in 1992, Dick, Mike, and I were all in the trials, the first time in history that three members of the same family competed. Unbelievably, Dick, at the age of thirty-six, skated well enough to make the trials again in 1994. He is a remarkable, remarkable athlete. He was also Mike's and my first coach, the first guy to really show us about gliding instead of just running on skates.

In a way, then, it was easiest for Mike and me. There was a standard of excellence already set, a Jansen skating tradition, by the time we started. There was also a nice, new outdoor rink in West Allis. So Mike and I could only roll our eyes when Dick would tell us about walking a mile in a snowstorm, shoveling off a pond, and then getting kicked off by the police when you were all done. I'm sure I'll have to invent something to tell Janie about how tough I had it, too.

My first pair of skates were double-runners, and my first real pair were hand-me-downs, probably from Dick. I was only four or five years old when I skated in my first pack-style meets. I'm told that both Mike and I preferred throwing snowballs and rolling down hills to actually competing, and the meet organizers used to bribe us with nickels and candy bars just to get us to the starting line. I was pretty successful from the beginning, though rarely the best. That honor belonged to Mike, who is about eighteen months older than I am. Most of the time we competed in different divisions, but he dominated his, whereas I was more like a second- or third-place skater. In the West Allis Speed Skating Club program the national outdoor pack-style champions from the club are listed. I'm mentioned once. Mike is in there four times.

There's a speed-skating circuit around Wisconsin, Minnesota, and Illinois, and from an early age Mike and I, just like Mary, Janet, and Dick before us, jumped right into it. At one time or another, my parents' entire weekend life was devoted to loading up the Volkswagen van, making sandwiches, packing sweaters, tying skates, and drying tears of disappointment. I don't know how they did it. By the time Mike and I really got into it, Mary and Janet were out of it, of course, but there was rarely a time when there weren't at least three Jansen kids competing.

How about this for a schedule? My father would come home on Friday night after working his four-to-midnight shift at the West Allis police department, and begin sharpening skates, sometimes three pairs, sometimes five. It would take him almost two hours. Meanwhile, my mother would be making peanut-butter-and-jelly sandwiches. Then they'd go to bed, maybe about 2:30, wake up at 5:30, and drive us all to Madison or Minneapolis or Chicago. Much of that time my father held another part-time job, too, driving a truck or landscaping or something like that. And my mom went back to work as a nurse from time to time. But they always had enough time to cart us around. Always. It was a way of life. And if the meet was on Sunday, you could add in a stop at church, too.

People always talked about how hard it must've been for my parents to watch me fail in the Olympics in '88 and '92. But hard didn't begin in 1988. Hard was putting on five layers of clothing to start the car at 5 A.M. for a four-hour drive. Hard was watching me stumble and fall and cry when I was ten years old. For my sisters, hard was convincing their boyfriends and husbands that where they wanted to be on a Sunday morning was watching some snot-nosed kid skate around a frozen pond. But that was just part of Jansen family life. If someone was doing something, the rest of the family was there. And it wasn't just sports—my sisters still remember getting up at 5 A.M. to watch Jim be an altar boy for the first time. Gee, sorry I missed that.

One memory from those early days sticks out. It was in 1977, when I was eleven years old and the national championship meet was in Minnesota. Mike won his division, his first national title, and I was in a good position to win mine. But coming around a turn in one of the races, I tripped on a rubber hose they had set up as a lane marker. (No jokes, please.) That slip cost me the national title by one point.

I started crying. I kept crying as my mom took off my skates, and I kept crying throughout the award ceremonies, and I kept crying when we got into the car, and I was still crying when we pulled into our driveway back in West Allis six hours later. I don't know why Mike, who shared the backseat with me, didn't kill me.

As we got out of the car, my father, who hadn't spoken a word to me all the way home, turned around and said, very quietly, "You know, Dan, there's more to life than skating in a circle."

Later in life, I came to truly know the importance of those words.

I don't think there's one prescribed way you become a champion. Pete Mueller, for example, who won a gold medal in the 1,000 in the 1976 Olympics, was a guy who did it largely on his own. He was an independent type who didn't need much support from his family and friends. But if I know anything, I know that having a large and supportive family in my corner has been the single most important plus in my career. Who knows why? But there have been times, maybe when I've been trailing in a race or faltering in my training, when I've literally been able to feel their strength and their collective will pushing me onward. I don't know whether I've ever thanked them properly for that, so that's what I'm doing now.

CHAPTER 3

Lillehammer

As I went through my mental checklist minutes before my 500-meter race, everything seemed to be in order. I'm not a particularly superstitious person, but I think every competitor in an individual sport gets accustomed to a certain routine and doesn't want to see it interrupted, least of all at the Olympics. Pete Mueller insisted on one thing—that during warm-ups I wear my Carolina Panthers hat, which he thought had become something of a good-luck charm. I just considered it good advertisement—Mark Richardson, who is one of the Panthers' owners, is married to Robin's sister Joan.

My routine essentially began the night before the race. I slept like a baby, which was a good sign. I've had good races after bad nights of sleep, as I had in the world championships several weeks earlier, but in general I need a solid seven or eight hours to feel really fresh. I arrived at the rink about 11 A.M., three hours before the race, and did the usual things to get loose—a little jogging, a little jumping around, lots of stretching, maybe forty-five minutes' worth. I got onto the ice, as usual, about ninety minutes before the race, did a few slow laps, some accelerations, a few starts. Every skater is out there doing essentially the same thing. I didn't say much of anything to anybody, and nobody said much to me. There wasn't anything to say.

I felt real good in the warm-up, which was also a good sign. When I came back off the ice, I noticed that my skates were still sharp so I didn't need to work on them. All that remained was to sit there for a long time alone, trying to relax, thinking.

Lots of things run through your mind, little scraps of memories, and I never let one linger too long—my sister Jane, Calgary in '88, Albertville in '92, all the fans back in Wisconsin who were pulling for me, my family. The main thought that I wanted to keep foremost in my mind was that I was the best 500-meter skater in the world. Nobody doubted that. If I could skate near the under-36 times that I had done in Hamar on December 4 (35.92) and then in Calgary on January 30 (35.76), I couldn't be beat. It was that simple. Even a week before the 500, I had turned in a hand-timed 35.9, which was easily the best of the field in that pre-Olympic tune-up. There was no one else capable of those kinds of races. So I had loads of confidence, and I think everyone around me did, too. "Let's get it on" was my philosophy.

The 500 was one of the first events in the Olympics, and for that reason I had skipped the opening ceremonies two days earlier. I had been told that there was an excellent chance I would've been elected to carry the flag, which would've been a great honor, but it was mitigated by the fact that athletes stand around for hours at the ceremonies and run the risk of cramping up. Missing the ceremonies was a small price to pay for being totally prepared for the race.

Before the race Pete had made about as positive a comment to the press as I ever heard any coach make: "I know Dan's going to win," he said. "The way he's skating, he can skate ninety percent and win. If he skates one hundred percent, he can win big. And right now he's skating a hundred and ten percent. He's the greatest sprinter in the history of speed skating, and he's going to prove it." Believe it or not, Pete's Muhammad Ali impression didn't bother me; I felt that confident, too.

My father didn't tell me this before the race, of course, but it was his opinion I would win the race because there was simply nothing bad left that could happen to me. In 1984 in Sarajevo, when I was an eighteen-year-old kid nobody knew, I had finished fourth, just sixteen hundredths of a second from a bronze, in the 500. After a personal tragedy in '88, I had fallen on a corner in the 500 and on a straightaway in the 1,000. In '92 I had run a slow race on slow ice in the 500, then burned myself out on good ice in the 1,000. Near-miss, tragedy, falls, slow ice, burnout. The only thing left was for the Zamboni to run over me on the last turn, and we just didn't think that would happen. Even Dr. Loehr was quietly optimistic. Unbeknown to me, he came to Norway (the first time he ever saw me compete live) to watch the 500 and booked his flight home for the following day, feeling that I would win and therefore wouldn't need his counsel for the 1,000.

That proves conclusively that you shouldn't always believe your doctor.

I did have some concern about the ice, though. The previous day I had told Dad that the ice had felt harder than it had all week, and that I wasn't gripping it as well. That was not good news for a power skater like myself because it meant that the ice could be brittle and break away. But I had pretty much put it out of my mind by race time.

After I finished my thinking, alone in the locker room, I got up, jogged a little more, took a couple spins on the stationary bike, came back to the locker room, and put on my skating uniform, which we call a skin. Then I slipped my bare feet (it just feels better that way) into my skates and laced them up. By 1:40 I was back onto the ice. I glanced briefly into the stands and thought about my family there—Robin, Jane, Mom and Dad, and my three oldest siblings, Mary, Janet, and Jim—but I didn't want to make eye contact. Too much to think about. Jane had the best attitude for the race, as I found out later. She was sleeping.

Strangely, I wasn't nearly as nervous as I had been before the world championships two weeks earlier. I'd really felt I needed a good race in Calgary to come into

Norway full of confidence, and I had gotten it. No one is better than you, D.J., I told myself. This is your time, D.J., I told myself. Go out and get what's yours, D.J., I told myself.

I was in the second pair of skaters, with Sean Ireland of Canada. I would've preferred to be later to get a real good idea of the ice, but that was simply the luck of the draw. In fact, I had been second pair in '88 and '92, too. I took my usual position right behind the first pair to get an idea of the starter. He issues three commands: go to the start, ready, and go. Even though each and every start is supposed to be the same, with a one-second pause between "ready" and "go," it doesn't always work out that way. So once in a while you can pick up a little advantage by listening to him. The first pair was a Chinese skater, Hongbo Liu, and a Canadian, Sylvain Bouchard. They were both good, but I didn't consider them my chief competition. But Bo ripped off a 36.54, which for him was quite good, and to me that was an indicator that the ice was fast.

That only reaffirmed my confidence that I could skate a sub-36. I felt at least a half-dozen skaters were capable of winning the race and coming close to breaking 36: the four Japanese, Horii, Miyabe, Hiroyasu

Shimizu, and Junichi Inoue, and two Russians, Aleksandr Golubev and Sergei Klevchenya. In retrospect, the no-holds-barred philosophy was a little risky because of the brittleness of the ice. But my feeling was that if I skated another world record, or close to it, I would win the gold because no one else was capable of doing it. Besides, the last thing I wanted to happen was to skate a safe speed and end up losing a slow race; that would've been absurd after what I had been through to try to win the gold.

Besides, working with Pete and with Dr. Loehr had uncovered an interesting little tidbit that I never would've realized on my own. My history in World Cup 500-meter races was to have a bad one the first time out, then come on strong in the second. We noticed it by looking at videotapes of my face. In the first race, I'd be out there with a calm look on my face, a real nice-guy demeanor about me, and I'd skate a mediocre time. Subconsciously, I knew I had another chance to skate well, and I usually did. But there's only one 500-meter race in the Olympics, so we decided to prepare for all my 500-meter races that season as if they were my only race. It had worked, and now I wanted to take that aggressive attitude to the line.

Finally, it was time. *Go to the start.* I took the line and prepared myself. I felt great, utterly focused on what I was doing. *Ready.* This was it. This was the moment when I threw off all the baggage. The race was being broadcast live back to the States in the morning, but that didn't bother me. It was medal time.

And then Sean false-started. No one should blame a race on a false start, but it certainly didn't help. There are times when you just feel real, real comfortable in your starting stance and you've got just the right toe-hold at the line, and you can't wait for that gun. This was one of those times. But I had to put it behind me and refocus. I didn't feel quite as comfortable after the restart, but I was still ready.

And then we were off.

I started on the inner lane and did the first 100 in 9.82 seconds, off my world-record interval of 9.75 but certainly good enough to win. But I wasn't gripping the ice very well. Perhaps I should've skated a more cautious race, but once you decide on a basic strategy it's foolish to back off it.

The best part of my race is usually the last 250 or 300 meters, so when I was still going strong at that point I knew I had an excellent chance for the gold. I was concentrating, feeling real good. But then, one or two strokes into my last turn, my left skate just kind of slipped and my hand touched the ice. Even with that momentary slip I felt that I still could've been in the race because I had some speed going. But I didn't grip the ice well on my next two strokes, either, and that killed it for me. I finished the race in 36.68, which is an incredibly fast time considering what happened. But they don't list "considering what happened"s when you get your time. If I hadn't slipped, I think my time would've been about 36.0 or 36.1. And had I crossed the finish line with that time, I know what I would've been thinking: "Good race, Dan, but not good enough for the gold." However, the gold-medal-winning time turned out to be 36.33. Even with the slip, I finished eighth and was only .35 of a second from winning the thing, which is absurd.

What happened? Well, it felt to me like the ice broke away, and that's what the replay seemed to show, too. If that was the case, there was nothing I could've done. I just couldn't seem to grip the ice right, and you need to "feel" a turn if you're going to put every ounce of strength into it. I never felt like my skates were digging in but, rather, just kind of riding on top. If it means anything, Roger Strøm of Norway fell at the same corner in the next pair.

On the other hand, if I would've just taken it a little easy instead of pushing too hard to get a time that no one else could touch, maybe it wouldn't have happened. Maybe I should've just been cruising and waiting until the second half of the turn to accelerate. I was on the outer lane for the final turn, which is when you generally do accelerate, but maybe I should've exercised more caution, taken a little more care around the turn, treated it like it was an inner turn.

Well, there was no shortage of analysis. Miyabe did suggest to the press that I had skated too aggressively on the last turn. Pete simply felt that what had happened with the ice was something that would never happen again. My good buddy Nick Thometz, who was out on the ice coaching other 500-meter skaters, thought that I'd looked tight, that I had made it through the first 200 meters fine but then had stopped relaxing and seemed to be chopping along rather than gliding. It didn't feel that way to me, but, who knows, maybe it was a condition of not feeling the ice very well.

But one fact stared me in the face: Once again, I had failed to medal. Once again, the unexpectedly horrible had happened to Dan Jansen. The gold medalist, Golubev, is a fine skater but one with a peculiar running style (he's a former hockey player) who rarely challenges me when I'm on my game. But I wasn't on my game. The sad saga of Dan Jansen and the Olympics continued.

When I crossed the finish line with that subpar time, it started a chain reaction of emotions all around me. Pete Mueller, I know, felt crushed. He said before the meet that there was a "void" in his coaching career that wouldn't be filled until I won a gold medal. His state of mind didn't keep him, however, from coming up with an all-time quip as he left the ice. A reporter asked him: "Was the ice slippery?" To which Pete responded: "Ice is always slippery." Up in the stands, Dr. Loehr felt like he should be at my side, and he started what turned out to be an arduous journey to be with me. The camera turned to Bonnie Blair—she was crying. Robin immediately turned and left, an action that was misinterpreted as her being mad at me or something, and she got the reputation, in some corners, as being a person who wasn't standing behind me. Absolutely ridiculous. She told me later that she had gotten so sick of seeing herself crying during my two races in Albertville—"That was like an Olympic event unto itself, Robin crying," she said—that she had to get away from the cameras. And when she did, of course, she started crying. It was just as hard on the others who were in Hamar, too, and the cameras registered their sadness time and time again.

This really worried my sister Mary because she was afraid, as Robin was, that it appeared the family was upset with me for not winning a medal. I certainly never thought that, but I'm sure others did. But my family's reaction sprang from much more complicated roots than pure disappointment. First of all, they felt bad for me. Not for themselves. For me. They knew how long and hard I had worked for a medal, and they knew how hard it was for me not to get it. And every time something bad happened at the Olympics it inevitably brought back, with a sudden stomach-wrenching rush, the memories of 1988 in Calgary, Jane's sickness and death, my two falls. It was just one gigantic storm cloud that kept showing up again and again, and there it was in Lillehammer. They weren't crying for one race—they were crying for what seemed to be almost a lifetime of disappointment and out-and-out tragedy that had come to be the Olympics for the Jansen family.

Back home, it was just as hard for my family. Diane was traveling in Wisconsin that day and watched the race, alone, in a hotel room. That must've been terrible. Mike said he woke up that morning, literally pumped up, feeling that this would be the day. Then he heard the phone ring and his little daughter say, "Daddy, Daddy, Uncle Dan slipped," and he got mad at her because he thought she was kidding around. Then he went to the breakfast table, saw a tear in the eye of his wife, Angie, and his day was ruined. He told me later that he kept saying over and over, "This can't be happening again. This can't be happening again."

Oh, it was. It really was. It's almost impossible to chronicle the truckload of emotions that was going through my mind. The first thing I did after the race was just kind of laugh to myself. It was the same kind of laugh that Sisyphus, the guy who kept pushing the rock up the hill only to watch it roll down again, must've laughed. The whole thing was just too ridiculous. Then Pete skated up and I looked him square in the eye and said, "I quit. I just plain quit." I didn't mean it literally, of course. Well, maybe for a second I did. When I went back in the locker room, two of my teammates, Dave Besteman and Nathaniel Mills, were getting ready for their 500s. I'm sitting there all depressed and talking about the ice and they're telling me how sorry they feel for me, and all of a sudden I said, "Guys, I'm sorry. You've got a race to get ready for. Stop thinking about me." They weren't serious medal contenders in the 500, but I felt bad about interrupting their prerace concentration.

I was asked to do an interview near the locker room, and for some reason I felt like talking. Who can explain it? I think, subconsciously, I just wanted everyone to know that I was all right and was not back in the locker room proclaiming the end of the world was near because I hadn't won a medal. After my 1992 500-meter race in Albertville I had lain around on the locker-room bench in shock for like an hour, and I didn't want to do that again. I even sought out a reporter from the Milwaukee paper, Dale Hofmann, and said to him, "Tell Milwaukee I'm sorry." I meant it, too.

The press stuff went okay, and then I saw Robin. Actually, she was on the phone with her sister and had forgotten our credit card number. Rather proudly, I rattled it off, demonstrating for perhaps the first time that afternoon that I could respond to pressure.

By that time, I got the word that the First Lady and some of the official delegation would like to meet with me.

"You wanna go see Hillary?" I asked Robin.

"Who's Hillary?" she asked.

Obviously she wasn't thinking too clearly by that time.

We met, and Mrs. Clinton extended her condolences, and everybody was really, really nice. I'm glad I did it. But after about ten minutes, it suddenly started to hit me, and I could see it was hitting Robin, too. The only way I could describe it was that I felt weird and disoriented. And then I felt a crushing, weighty sadness. It was the sadness of realization. *I would never win a medal in the 500 meters. Maybe I was the best ever, but my chance at a medal was gone. Forever.* I knew Robin was thinking the same thing and feeling bad for me, and then I started feeling bad for her for feeling so bad about me. When you're alone with someone you love, that's when you feel it the worst because you feel for each other. Then Pete came in, and that turned it into an official three-way cry. I knew how hard he had worked for this and how badly he wanted it for me. That was good for another three or four minutes of tears.

Then I saw my family, and by then I was finished with my crying. Every once in a while I'd get the urge, but I fought it off. Eventually, Dr. Loehr worked his way down to visit me, having set a new Olympic record for dodging security men and ducking into illegal places, and I was in utter shock to see him. His visit helped a lot. I was supposed to do another press conference, this one a major deal with all the reporters, but Dr. Loehr strongly advised against it.

"You have got to start preparing for the thousand," he told me. "You've got to put the five hundred behind you immediately and stop reliving it."

I wasn't sure what to do. Dr. Loehr was absolutely correct in his assessment. There was a general feeling in the Jansen camp that in Albertville in 1992 I had blown my preparation time between the 500 and the 1,000, and I didn't want to do the same thing this year. His idea was not to let me grieve about the 500 or dwell on it in any way, shape, or form. It was over and done with, and now it was time to concentrate on the 1,000. On the other hand, I realized that the press had a job to do and I didn't want to be considered a guy who was ducking comment after the bad times. Considering what I had gone through in the previous two Olympics, I don't know how they could've thought that, but you never know. But I decided to go with the doc's advice. I sent my apologies, and the Olympic officials understood.

Later, I found out that a television crew had waited for me for two hours outside in subzero temperatures and one of the cameramen had suffered frostbite as a result. I sent him an apology over the Olympic electronic mail system, but I didn't feel real good about it.

My choice of venues for the night—my cramped cell of a room in the Olympic Village or the house that my family had rented—was a no-brainer. I hadn't spent a lot of time over at the house, because I needed peace and quiet before the race, but now I needed the love and support I could get only from my family. I talked to Dr. Loehr from time to time, hugged Robin and Janie, played cribbage with my father and Jim. Outwardly, everything was back to normal. Inwardly, it was horrible because I couldn't shake the feeling.

I'm probably the best ever, but I am not going to win an Olympic medal in the 500 meters.

That night I dozed off fairly easily because I was so tired. But about 3 A.M. I woke up and just couldn't get back to sleep. I woke up Robin, and we talked and cried and talked some more. We dozed off for a little while, and I woke up at 7 A.M. Jane was sleeping in the crib next to us, and, as a small but much-needed stroke of fate, she happened to be waking up just as I looked in at her. She peered over the crib and gave me the most wonderful smile I've ever seen.

Well, I thought, the world will go on, after all.

INTERLUDE III

A Full-Time Commitment

You give up a lot when you dedicate yourself full-time to a sport. And in the quiet times I often think about how different my life would've been had I not decided that my happiness lay in racing around a refrigerated oval. Actually, I have no real answers because I can't imagine myself doing anything else. Most of the Jansens are either policemen or nurses. The former seemed like a good job when I was young, but that was mainly because my father was a cop and I was proud of him. And as for nursing, I just don't think the uniform would look right on me. The truth is, I love skating and I've always loved it. The public has seen the sport be cruel to me, dangle success in front of me before snatching it away at the last moment. But the public doesn't see those quiet times of pure joy, either, the joy of the perfect workout, the joy of sharing a goal with my fellow competitors, the joy of living up to and exceeding one's own expectations. So I have no regrets about what I chose to do.

But that doesn't stop me from thinking.

Certainly I would've gone farther in other sports than I did had I not dedicated myself to skating. I think I could've been a fairly good football player, maybe not a top Division I prospect but definitely college material as either a running back or safety. My high school football career actually got an unexpected jump start when I was in ninth grade and still at Frank Lloyd Wright Junior High. This sounds like a made-up story, but it's absolutely true. A bunch of my friends on the football team decided to do some drinking one night, which is one thing, but the site they chose was the lawn of the junior high, which is quite another. I happened to be watching Mike play a junior varsity football game that night, once again proving that in life timing is everything. As for the question of whether or not I would've been there if I'd had the opportunity, I just don't know. At any rate they all got caught, and the principal decided to disband the junior high team. He let myself and the four or five others who hadn't been there go up and play on the junior varsity team, however, and I ended up doing pretty well. Then, as a sophomore, I got a lot of playing time and the coach was definitely counting on me for my last two years. But skating got in the way.

I did play all three years of high school baseball and had pretty good success as an infielder. I read somewhere that I was a major league prospect but if that's true I really wasn't aware of it. I suspect I was like a million other decent high school players—good speed, good head for the game, good fielder, but probably not good enough at the plate to hit major league pitching.

Socially, I missed some things, too. The best part of high school is fall weekends, homecoming, hay rides, dances, those kinds of things, and for my junior and senior years I was away training much of the time. I was around for the proms, but in some ways I guess I was somewhat of a mystery guy around West Allis Central, the kid who took off for some godforsaken place in Europe just when the school year got interesting.

My grades were always good, nearly all A's in the lower grades and mostly A's and B's in high school. Well, there was one exception. When I was a senior I got an F in advanced algebra. There were extenuating circumstances. I wrote down the questions of a test for my girlfriend at the time, and the teacher found out about it. In my defense, he always gave different tests, so I really didn't look upon it as cheating but, rather, just helping out. As it turned out, my girlfriend needed even more help than I suspected, because she pulled out the list of questions during the test. I pleaded my case, but the teacher wouldn't listen. F for the quarter. And I eventually got a new girlfriend.

I was pretty forthright about taking my books on the road with me and kept up with the work. If I have one regret academically, though, it's that I sometimes took an easy course over a difficult one and didn't really challenge myself. I suspect I have that in common with 90 percent of American males in high school. My mother was happy enough with my report cards, but she used to gag when she got to the Days Absent column. "You know, Dan, employers who ask for high school transcripts sometimes only look at the attendance records," she'd say. Fortunately, Mom, I never had to worry about it.

My strongest feeling of regret came late in my senior year, when most of my friends were getting ready to go to college at the University of Wisconsin or Marquette and talking about classes and cars and girls. I never actually sat down and said to myself, "You're not going to college," but that's the way it worked out. The year I graduated from high school was 1983. Instead of college, my thoughts were on the '84 Olympics.

—

What you have to understand about speed skating is that it's kind of a universe unto itself. It's not like Little League baseball or Pop Warner football in that all your friends are playing or coming to watch you play. It's a sport with only isolated pockets of interest. There are maybe fifty kids from Wisconsin, forty kids from Minnesota, thirty kids from Chicago showing up at the same weekend meets, so you get to know one another very well. These kids who at first seem so strange to you gradually become your friends. Their parents are making the same sacrifices your parents are making to haul you around to meets. They're going through the same hard training regimen as you are. They've made the same commitment to this strange, nearly anonymous sport that you have. You're kind of like those people in Spielberg's *Close Encounters of the Third Kind,* drawn together by almost mystical forces.

All that is a fancy way of saying that in skating I made

very special friends, right from the beginning, and that's a major reason I stuck with it. In my case, one of those friends was my brother Mike. The others were people like John Baskfield, Andy Gabel, and Nick Thometz. We began competing against one another when we were eight or nine years old, and we're still best of friends twenty years later. I'm not saying that's unprecedented in sports, but it's certainly unusual. And there was a cute little girl at those meets so long ago who also became one of our group. Her name was Bonnie Blair.

The point I'm making is that whatever friendships and activities I missed in my own area because of skating, I more than made up for. Maybe I felt a moment's sadness at not playing intramural basketball on Saturday mornings in sixth grade, but I knew that at that meet in Whitefish Bay or someplace I'd run into the two Minnesota kids, Nick and J.B., or that funny kid from the Chicago area, Andy Gabel, called Gabes. It was those kinds of relationships that kept me in the sport.

It certainly wasn't my overwhelming success. I was always among the top skaters, but generally, between the ages of, say, nine and twelve, Gabes and J.B. beat me most of the time. (And, as I said before, my brother was having a lot of success in the division right above me, in which he competed against Nick.) Whenever we talk about it now, J.B. and Gabes won't let me forget it. "You were nothing." "You were toast." Those are some of the nicer things they tell me.

I don't know what kept me going. The pure joy of it, partly. I loved being outside in the winter, the wind in my face, the sun reflecting off the ice, all that snow piled up. I'm sure I didn't look at it quite so poetically then, but it was a feeling that always got me pumped. In fact, a part of me is almost sorry that indoor tracks became popular. Sure, the ice is easier to control in most cases and bad weather isn't so much of a factor, but the feeling of being outside, close to the elements, is missing. The funny thing is, Rick Smith remembers walking to school with me and all we did was complain about the cold weather. But once I laced up the skates the cold didn't matter.

Somebody once said about being a writer that you don't choose writing; it chooses you. I guess it's the same with skating. Something inside me knew that that's what I wanted to do. Same thing with Nick. Same thing with Gabes. Take my brothers Dick and Mike. They were great, great skaters, but the sport just didn't tap them on the shoulder as hard as it did me. So they didn't make quite the same commitment.

It wasn't always easy. I remember we started summer training when I was about fourteen years old, and I ached to be playing baseball or swimming in the pool instead of duckwalking or running wind sprints. But I ignored the temptations. Pete Mueller always says that out of 100 people with skating talent, 99 aren't willing to make the commitment to do the work. I'm sure aficionados of every sport could come up with some number like that, but I'm also sure that the percentage is much more dramatic in a sport like speed skating, where the public recognition is so limited. And I want to emphasize again that no one was pushing me into skating, least of all my father. It was my decision. I wasn't the only kid in West Allis with a poster of Eric Heiden and the 1976 Olympic speed-skating team on my wall, instead of the Green Bay Packers or Milwaukee Brewers, but I was certainly one of the few.

Oh, man, Eric Heiden! He was the man. Eric won his five gold medals in the 1980 Olympics when I was fourteen, but even before that he was a world champion, and there he was working out at the West Allis rink. I was in awe. He'd be sitting on the bench lacing up his skates or just resting, and I'd kind of inch my way over to within ten feet of him. I remember wondering if he knew who I was. He probably did, but only as the squirt brother of Dick Jansen or one of my older sisters.

When I was about fourteen, I started to grow, and all of a sudden I was the one winning most of the time. That kept me going, motivated me, and made me even more sure of what I wanted to do. So before my junior year I went up and told my father, "Dad, I want to quit football and concentrate on skating." His response was typically verbose.

"Okay," he said.

I'm pretty sure that, under oath, my father would admit to having had a minor regret that I was giving up a game that he loved. But he truly wanted what I wanted.

I don't remember that my decision was a particularly big moment in the life of the Jansen family. No trumpets, no flags at half-mast, no special meal at home. Even to my own way of thinking, the most significant part of my decision was that I was quitting football, not that I was joining the society of speed skaters. But in retrospect it was my personal crossing of the Rubicon, no doubt about it. Deep inside me, maybe deeper than I realized, lay the belief that I could become a champion if I dedicated myself fully to skating.

It certainly changed my life rather drastically. For at least six weeks I left high school, in October and November, to train in Europe. That idea came from Pete Mueller, who was by then involved in coaching our national team. Pete's theory was that only by experiencing firsthand the rigors of international travel and competition could young skaters develop, and he couldn't have been more correct. (And besides, in those days we didn't have ice back home until November.) During much of the school year, my classes were arranged so I could leave at two o'clock to work out at State Fair Park. That would last about two hours, after which I'd come home, do my homework, eat dinner, and go back to the rink for an evening session.

Who knows what would have happened if a teacher or a principal had said, "No way that kid's missing that much school"? I was young and my parents weren't the kind of people to really challenge authority, so maybe I wouldn't have gotten in all this extra training and I wouldn't have gotten to the top. What you have to remember is that, for a kid, being the starting tailback at

West Allis Central was still a lot cooler than being a national-class speed skater. The school was really nice about announcing my accomplishments when I'd return from some faraway competition, but I'm sure half the students had no idea that winning a junior world meet actually had any meaning. I knew that, but I didn't care. This sport was my future.

I was a sophomore in high school when I went to Europe for the first time. I think every kid competing internationally initially assumes that he's going to get his butt kicked. Part of my motivation for training so hard came from the thought that the Russians must be working out twenty-three hours a day and drinking some kind of Soviet vitamin concoction that would give them superhuman strength. Bonnie had the same situation with the East German girls, although considering what's been revealed over the last few years about their steroid use, Bonnie probably was right to worry. But then I discovered that the best Americans were as good as the best Europeans. The first time I competed overseas, in Davos, Switzerland, I set a junior world record of 38.24 in the 500 meters. I didn't even know there *was* a junior world record, but I was glad to have it. My family chipped in and bought me a ring with the time inscribed on it.

We didn't realize it then, but it was an amazing group of juniors that came along about that time. When Eric Heiden was competing as a junior, for example, he swept through the competition, just like he did at the '80 Olympics. But we had any number of guys who could win. The East German skater, Uwe-Jens Mey, who eventually became a good friend of mine, was competing. Igor Zhelezovsky from the Soviet Union. Nick Thometz. Myself. We all eventually became Olympic rivals; heck, Igor was one of the guys I beat in Lillehammer.

In World Cup competitions you skate all different distances, not just your speciality. In the juniors, for example, you skate 500, 1,500, 3,000, and 5,000 meters. In the 1983 junior world championships I was in third place overall after the first three distances, then went out and set a personal record in the 5,000. You know what it got me? Ninth place. I finished six places lower because my 5,000 was so bad compared to the best of the field. I think the best international performance I ever had outside of the 500 and the 1,000 was a seventh place in the 1,500. If I wasn't 100 percent sure I wanted to concentrate on the shorter distances before I went to Europe, I certainly was after gauging myself in the longer races. These days, by the way, there's probably even more specialization. There are some Japanese skaters who concentrate on the 500 meters and don't even skate the 1,000. I don't think there will ever again be a skater to come along who will do what Eric Heiden did, which is to dominate all the distances. I may be the fastest, but he's still the best speed skater who's ever lived.

When I made my first junior world team in 1983, there was a little surprise around my hometown. "You mean Dan made it instead of Mike?" I heard a few people say. It didn't really surprise me because this was right around the time that I was starting to beat Mike regularly. Remember that he had kept on playing high school football and didn't really train as seriously as I did. And, then, in the Olympic trials, I qualified for both the 500 and the 1,000. *That* really surprised a lot of people, that this eighteen-year-old kid was actually going to the Olympics. But only my family, my close friends in skating, and I truly knew how hard I had been working. And, tell you the truth, I would've been surprised if I *hadn't* made that team.

What you have to remember is that Eric Heiden had thrown things out of whack by winning five golds at Lake Placid, and though the rest of the team was very good, only two others had won medals. Nick, Bonnie, and I and a couple others considered ourselves the new breed, the successors to Eric, the building blocks of the future. We knew we probably wouldn't show it at Sarajevo, but it represented our first step to build a truly strong American speed-skating team, one that could dominate the Games in 1988. There's a famous picture in my mom's scrapbook, famous because it's so comical. Nick and I are posed together holding some small camera that Kodak gave us for making the '84 Olympic team. Nick has his Prince Valiant haircut, and I look like I'm about ten years old. I look at that photo sometimes, and it gives me a lot of perspective about how far I've come and how long I've been doing this.

The Sarajevo Games were everything I thought they would be. I'm eighteen years old, the youngest skater at the Games and one of the youngest athletes in any sport, and there's Scott Hamilton, the figure skater, sitting across from me, wishing me luck. It was almost too much to imagine. My parents came over to watch, and I know they were thrilled. I felt proud because after all those weekend drives to outposts like Appleton and Waupaca, I could finally reward them with a trip to a place like Sarajevo. When I think what's happened to that city since then and contrast it with my memories of a romantic, almost magical place, I almost start to cry.

On the day of my 500-meter race, which was scheduled for nine in the morning, it started to snow and kept on snowing. The race was moved back until late that afternoon—remember, it was an outdoor venue at that time—but it didn't bother me that much. I had skated through many snowstorms at the West Allis rink, and I was pretty good at making adjustments. I just wanted to skate a good race, no matter what the conditions. I remember thinking as I took the line how much less nervous I was than I had been at the trials. Making the team was the main thing; this was simply icing on the cake. And, partly because of that attitude, I skated a wonderful race, 38.55, that put me in third place. Most people figured I would be doing well with a top-ten finish, but, tell you the truth, I felt deep inside that I could win a medal. However, when Gaétan Boucher of Canada came along and beat my time to take away the bronze, I wasn't crushed. Gaétan was a great skater who would later win both the 1,000 and the 1,500. There would be other medal chances for Dan Jansen, I thought to myself. I had proven myself among the best in the world and more than justified my decision to take up the sport full time. I didn't skate as well in the 1,000, but then I didn't expect to, and I finished a reasonable sixteenth. Nick did even better than I did. He was fifth in the 500, only one hundredth of a second behind me, and also took a fourth in the 1,000. We didn't have a medal to show, but the new breed would be ready to take over in '88. (Or so we thought.)

When I got home from the Olympics that year, however, I realized for the first time the lure and power of the Olympic medal. My thinking was: You're eighteen years old and you're the fourth best in the world. Wow! My family thought the same way. I truly believe my brother Jim when he tells me that he was never more proud of me than when I got fourth in Sarajevo. Well, maybe in Lillehammer. But most everyone else's thought was: "Jeez, you just missed getting a medal. Bummer, man!" That kind of attitude is antithetical to any reasonable perception of what competition is all about. I missed a bronze by sixteen hundredths of a second, and for that I should feel bad?

Looking back, I suppose the '84 Games in Sarajevo

were my only "pure" Olympics. I went there with low expectations and high principles. Not too many people knew the name of Dan Jansen, and, honestly, the only thought I had in my mind was to compete as well as I could. If I got a medal, fine; if I didn't, that was fine, too.

To say the least, the Olympics were never that simple again.

CHAPTER 4

Lillehammer

● FEBRUARY 15, 1994

The day after. I woke up with a much better feeling than I had after losing the 500s in both 1988 and '92. "If I could do it all over again today," I told Robin, "I would win that race." I wouldn't have said that after the 500 in either Calgary or Albertville. Then again, that thought, along with seven kroner, would've gotten me a few sticks of salmon jerky on the streets of Lillehammer.

The first step in preparing for my final Olympic race would be simple: I would get my butt over to the rink to practice. That sounds elementary, but it wasn't. After I'd lost the 500 in Albertville, I'd done something of a Howard Hughes impression, playing hooky from practice, hanging around with Robin, feeling a bit sorry for myself instead of trying to generate positive feelings about the upcoming 1,000-meter race. It was both Pete's and my fault, mostly mine. Pete was devastated and angry after I failed to win the 500. "Just go blow out the thousand," he said and really didn't offer much of a strategic prerace plan. Perhaps he sensed that it would've fallen on deaf ears anyway. I was a defeated hombre even before the race and didn't do the things I needed to do to prepare adequately. Dr. Loehr tried to lift my spirits by telephone, but he couldn't pull me out of the psychological hole I had dug for myself. He's never told me this, but I'd be willing to bet that the memory of the frustrating calls he'd made to Albertville was the major reason he came to Norway.

So I was determined that 1994 was not going to be a repeat of 1992. And had I shown even the slightest indication that I was going to flake out on my preparation, both Pete and Dr. Loehr would've dragged me bodily over to the arena. Robin might've too. And for all I know, baby Jane might've kicked me out. But none of them had to. I'm not saying it was the easiest thing in the world, but I knew what had to be done. Pete and Dr. Loehr were there with me every step of the way, too.

A big part of my willingness to prepare for the 1,000 was that I honestly thought I had a chance to win it. Despite my work with Dr. Loehr, neither Pete nor I had felt that way in '92, which was, of course, a sure sign that I wouldn't win. My 1,000-meter season before Albertville simply had not been strong enough. But with three World Cup wins before Lillehammer, I knew I had the right stuff to be a factor in 1994.

Pete could draw parallels to his own situation. In 1976, he had also skated a poor race in the 500, but he'd come back, in somewhat of a surprise, to win the 1,000. Wouldn't it be fitting, we both thought, if I could do the same thing?

Dr. Loehr had his own take on the situation, and he began talking to me about it. *What an unbelievable triumph this would be, Dan, if you could win this 1,000. Just when everybody's counted you out, Dan, now's the time to surprise everybody in a positive way. There's no reason you can't resurrect your courage and fight one more time, Dan, and the enormity of your victory would be all the more. Winning the 500, your specialty, wouldn't be the best end-*

ing to your story, Dan. This would be the best ending. Positive thoughts. He wouldn't let anything else into my mind.

The diabolical irony that the 1,000 would represent my last chance at an Olympic medal did not escape any of us, of course. For the better part of ten years the 1,000 had been kind of like the second-best suit in my closet. The 500 was the beautiful blue pinstripe, the one I pulled out for all the special occasions because I knew it looked good. The 1,000 was there only because I needed a suit for the off days, something to wear when I thought it was going to rain. For the longest time I just hadn't believed in the 1,000, and the reasons were both psychological and physiological. Oh, I'd thrown in some real good 1,000s from time to time, just to tempt me and establish the fact that I couldn't be counted out in any race. And had I been a more arrogant person, I suppose I could've convinced myself that I was the world's best in both the 500 and the 1,000. But something stopped me.

The mental aspect aside, there are substantial differences between the distances. Over the last decade I had come to believe that my style was simply a 500 style. I skated the corners with good technique—as I had proven the day before, you can rarely afford even the most minor slip in the 500—and I had the speed to get off the line. In simplest terms, I just flat out *overpowered* that race from start to finish. But the 1,000 had an endurance factor that, for me, always seemed to kick in with about 200 meters left. Putting the races in track terms, which might be easier to understand, I did not consider the 500 and the 1,000 like the 100 meters and the 200 meters for sprinters. There is no reason why a great 100-meter man cannot also be a great 200-meter man. A closer comparison is the 200 meters and the 400 meters. They are really different races, the former a pure explosion of power, the latter a kind of controlled sprint that is far more exhausting. Rarely in track is a good 200-meter sprinter also a great 400-meter man.

Then again, perhaps that analysis was flawed and the only reason I became fatigued at a certain point in the 1,000 was that I *expected* to get fatigued. Maybe my failure to dominate the 1,000 was in fact a self-fulfilling prophecy based on my resistance to the event. There is one school of thought that a skater will always be best competing one distance above where he thinks he'll be best—the great philosopher Andy Gabel told me that—but for the longest time I didn't buy it.

I tossed all these things around in my head as I talked to Dr. Loehr at practice. When I first went to see him in the spring of 1991, I had decided, with Pete's urging, to make improving my performance in the 1,000 one of my goals. It was most definitely the secondary one; as I said before, getting the negative thoughts about 1988 out of my mind in time for Albertville was foremost. But they were more interconnected than I thought. What I came to realize was that my failure in the 1,000 in Calgary weighed on me much more heavily than the 500. There is no way in the world I could've won the 500 on the very day that my sister died. But the 1,000 went off four days later, after I'd had time to absorb my loss. Further, I had dedicated the race to Jane. And when I failed in my attempt, I suffered an enormous, subconscious sense of guilt. Not only was I absent when Jane died, selfishly pursuing my own dreams and hopes of glory, but I also failed to give her what I had secretly promised—victory in the 1,000. It took me a long time to work through these negative thoughts. But I did it.

Dr. Loehr and I laughed about my reaction when he first told me how he wanted to approach the goal of improving my 1,000s. "Now, you're gonna think this is crazy . . ." he began. And he was right. I'm making this incredibly simplistic, of course, but Dr. Loehr's belief was that the more a person confronted a personal demon and made it part of his daily life, the better his chance of defeating it. Dr. Loehr had worked with several tennis players, one of whom had an intense fear, even hatred, of tiebreakers. He was a great player until he got himself into a tiebreaker, at which point he turned into a hacker who couldn't win at the public courts. So Dr. Loehr had him write "I love tiebreakers." And, sure enough, one night Dr. Loehr got the call he wanted to hear: "I was in a tiebreaker today, Doc, and guess who won?"

And so there I was, like some first-grade schoolkid, writing "I love the 1,000" every single day. I put it on my training charts, right at the top of the page. I had a note in my little drawer in the bathroom, the one with my razor and all that stuff. I'm not sure Robin even saw that one. I had a 1,000 note on the refrigerator and one on the bedroom mirror. "I love the 1,000" became my personal mantra, and you've got to admit it has more pop than "Ommmmm."

I was aware, of course, that in part I was playing a game with myself. But that's part of the concept. You start out with cynicism. Hey, I love the 1,000. Ha, ha. It doesn't happen overnight, but maybe you finally do win one and you laugh about that note you wrote on hotel stationery before the race. Then you win another. And you see another note. And it becomes like a game. Then you win another. Hey, maybe I really *do* love the 1,000. Maybe there's something to this.

But there was much more that went into my improvement at the distance. And the guy in the dark shades and the jean jacket charting my lap times was a big part of that "so much more." Dr. Loehr took care of the mind. Pete Mueller definitely took care of the body. Most people would say that Pete and I are proof that opposites attract, and there is some truth to that. But what we have in common is so much more important—a passion for speed skating. Neither of us cares about the politics or the economics of the sport or the way things appear to outsiders. We find joy in the effort, purity in the competition.

I can't remember when Pete and I first met, but it was very early in my career. He was one of my heroes when I was young because of his victory in the 1,000 in the 1976 Olympics. He always jokes that his wife, Leah Poulos Mueller, is the real skater in the family because she won three silver medals and a couple of world championships whereas he just got lucky once. But in truth he was a ferocious, ferocious competitor. He once told me that from the time he saw an American skater get an Olympic medal, when he was a little boy, all he wanted to do was be an Olympian. He worked with single-minded pursuit toward that goal, and he achieved it.

Pete was very much a technician, too. His theory with young skaters is that strength can be developed but technique, a basic "feel" for the ice, must be present to some degree or it's going to be difficult to build a champion sprinter. Even when I was twelve or thirteen years old and hardly the dominant skater in my division, Pete saw my potential, encouraged me, and took a special interest in whatever I was doing. You don't forget that when you're a kid, and we built a special relationship that, ultimately, had a lot to do with my success.

Pete would've probably been my Olympic coach in 1984 except that he had spent the previous year trying to make a comeback as a competitor. He didn't make it, but two of the kids he had been working with, Thometz and Jansen, did. Pete got into program development after that and eventually left the country to coach the West German national team.

Toward the end of the 1990–91 season, Bonnie,

Nick, and I decided that what we needed was Pete Mueller back in the United States. The season had been in many respects the most disappointing of our careers. Nick was still competing at that point even though a blood disorder had limited his effectiveness, but he was still passionately interested in what was best for skating. And both Bonnie and I felt that we were at a competitive standstill. I was doing okay, but I just felt like there was much more inside of me that wasn't getting out. The national team coach in '88, Mike Crowe, was a wonderful technician, but, for me personally, he was not the ideal coach. He was not a driving, motivating type of guy, and that's what I needed. After Mike, the job went to John Teaford, and he was unable to draw out our best. It's not absolutely crucial that a coach be a former Olympic-level competitor. But if you get one of those types who also happens to be a good technician and a motivator, then you've really got something. That describes Pete Mueller. So this self-appointed committee of three talked to Pete and twisted some arms in the United States International Speed Skating Association to see if we could get it done.

If that kind of thing sounds out of character for me, it was. I don't like to speak out, and I certainly don't like political power plays. Neither do Bonnie and Nick. But we all felt it was something that was desperately needed.

There were two problems. First, Pete was under contract to the West German national team, which expected him to lead them into the '92 Games. When we saw Peter at the season's final World Cup race in Inzell, West Germany, and asked him to come back, his response was: "I'd love to. My heart and soul is with you guys. But I don't think they'll let me out." And, second, Pete was the person least likely to win a popularity contest sponsored by the speed-skating association. Saying that Pete goes his own way is like saying that Madonna goes her own way, and his independent streak often turned people off. But one of the advantages of not speaking out very often is that you're taken pretty seriously when you do. And we finally did convince the reluctant USISA that Pete should have the job.

Fortunately, the Germans took a reasonable position. They wouldn't have let Pete out for any other country, but it just wasn't right, they said, to keep a man from his homeland. They could've played hardball but they didn't, and I know Pete will never forget their kindness.

Pete's philosophy is simple: You can't get too strong, and you can't have too much endurance. You would not believe how hard we worked—long runs, eight to twelve miles, duckwalking up hills again, in-line skating, non-stop tough, tough training. I can tell you that in those early months he was called a lot more than "Pete." Did I agree with everything he did? No, I didn't. I think he went overboard on the endurance stuff from time to time. Our summer training in Calgary that first year he came back was like nothing I've ever seen, something tantamount to boot camp. We'd get on the ice and do an endurance workout, sixty laps or something like that. Or we'd do what Pete called a "continuous workout," which was thirty minutes of nonstop stuff on the ice, maybe four laps hard, two laps easy, work the turns hard, then do a few easy ones. So while you do get a little aerobic rest, you're also down in skating position all the time, and, man, your back is just on fire. Then we'd get off the ice, drive immediately to this steep, steep ski hill, and run or duckwalk up it two, three, four times. It didn't matter how many times, really, because you were literally delirious with fatigue anyway. And then he'd have you do a nice little forty-five-minute endurance run back to the dorm.

We'd make little comments about hopping into a cab and Pete would laugh, but we knew that he expected us to stick it out, and we did. Keep in mind now that in competition we skate a maximum of about 1 minute, 15 seconds in a 1,000-meter race, and a 500 lasts about half that long. Granted, this kind of work was going on six months before the Olympics, so it's not like it was going to kill us for Albertville. But my problem was that I didn't think we needed *that* much of an endurance base. I sometimes felt like I was training for the Boston Marathon instead of a speed-skating race. Maybe some of Pete's philosophy came from the era of Eric Heiden, who was such an animal that he did all this stuff with ease. But not everyone is Eric Heiden. And some of it came from the fact that Pete had been working mostly with endurance skaters over the past few years.

Look, coaching is an art, not a science. There is no exact map or book to follow, and there is no way that an athlete is going to agree with his coach in every situation. You put two people together, but there's no precise measure to gauge if they are going to click. Bonnie, for example, eventually decided to split with Pete, and for the '94 Olympics she was coached by none other than Nick Thometz. But on balance, nobody could've done for me what Pete Mueller did.

I know a lot of the endurance stuff he had me do was

part of an overall plan to improve my performance in the 1,000. What Pete had to convince me of—and he finally did—was that hard training for the 1,000 would not hurt me in the 500. I didn't believe that at first, and neither did a lot of other people who told me I would screw up my 500 by improving my 1,000. Pete was positive I wouldn't. He equated it to a half-miler in track becoming a good miler. He would never hurt his half-mile time with the harder endurance training. Pete reasoned, he would only help his mile. The message eventually got through.

Another positive quality of Pete's is that he does not overcoach technique, and his feedback when I'm skating was always very positive, comments like "Hey, looks great, you're unbelievable, you're the best." Come to think of it, he may have been doing on the ice exactly what Dr. Loehr was doing off it. And as our relationship grew, he also came to trust my instincts more. If I would suggest that maybe I wouldn't have to do that final four- to six-mile run, he'd say okay. By the time Lillehammer rolled around, we were the best team in the world.

Of course, I didn't show it in the 500 meters. But there was still one more chance.

Disappointment and heartbreak did not begin for me at the 1988 Olympics. As I said before, it's hard for most Americans to imagine that we speed skaters are actually doing something besides trying out for the Olympics or competing in the Olympics, but there is a whole series of World Cup and World Sprint meets in the "off years." And I really think that some of the injuries and personal setbacks I had to recover from early in my career, when no one was watching, ultimately prepared me for those times when I later failed and the *whole world* was watching.

It might be helpful to explain a little bit about a skater's life, at least the way it was for me throughout the 1980s. Beginning in the summer months, you try to get your base endurance training down with physical work at home. In the fall, maybe about the first of October, you leave for Europe because the ice is ready there at least six weeks before it is in America. You stay there to train, compete in the first couple World Cup meets of the season, and return home at the end of November.

You spend Christmas at home and return to Europe on or about New Year's Day because the first World Cup race of the new year is usually in the first or second week of January. Then you spend the rest of the season in Europe and come home again in the spring to a glorious ticker-tape parade. Just kidding. You come home and everybody says, "So, Dan, what have you been up to?" The schedule got a little easier after the Pettit Center opened up because now the American skaters could get onto the ice in September and stay home until the European competitions.

It's funny, but probably the closest I ever felt to chucking the sport and finding something else to do with my life was not after the '88 or '92 Olympics. It was during the 1984–85 season, a few months after Sarajevo. First, I pulled a hamstring while jogging, one of the worst injuries for a speed skater. Then, while I was rehabilitating my leg on the Cybex machine, I pulled the *other* one. The only reason I had the good leg strapped in there was to keep it strong. Maybe right then and there I should've said to myself, "Dan, I don't think you're the luckiest guy in the world."

Trying to speed-skate with two bad hamstrings is like trying to fry hamburgers with two broken thumbs. You just can't do it. Week after week I limped around, getting weaker and weaker because I couldn't do any strength work with my legs. I didn't get onto the ice until October but went over to Germany to train anyway. One of the toughest things for a nineteen-year-old kid is watching teammates like Nick Thometz doing three workouts a day, getting strong, getting better, while you're sitting back in your room, watching movies, half of which are in German. So I came home and moped around, and by this time even my father was getting frustrated. That's when the thought crossed all of our minds that maybe I should find something else to do. But it didn't last long. Gradually, my hamstrings started to get better and I was at maybe 70 percent in December, when the trials for the world teams were held in Milwaukee.

Ironically, not being in peak form for those races really taught me something. I was still afraid of pulling a muscle in the 500, so I didn't use the customary running start to build up speed. I just started skating right off the line, built up my speed gradually, and won the race. It really taught me the virtue of taking long, powerful strides. I remember that Pete Mueller, who was not my coach at the time, came over and told me, "Dan, this is a blessing in disguise." I'm not suggesting that style alone is going to win an Olympic race. My time was about 38.2 or so, which these days isn't that great. But it wasn't that bad, either, and it proved to me that leg speed isn't everything.

I went on to get a silver medal in the 500 at the world sprints in 1985. And though I can't compare it to what later happened at Lillehammer, it was a really big moment for me, my first world championship medal when I was only nineteen. Moreover, it taught me another valuable lesson. Only a couple of months after a deeply discouraging period in my life, I was able to turn it into something positive through perseverance.

In 1986, the year after my hamstring problems, I really started to come into my own as a skater. I won a medal in every race that year and also became the first American to go under 37 seconds in the 500. I finished first in both the 500 and 1,000 in the World Cup standings, clinching them in the final race of the season in Inzell, West Germany. My parents had been able to come over and watch the race, and my brother Mike was still competing and was there, too. Before the banquet where I was going to receive my hardware, Mike and Nick Thometz and a couple other guys were back in my room playing poker—penny-ante poker, to be sure. Man, it didn't get any better than this. Family, friends, a first in the World Cup. I was feeling on top of the world.

So I should've known something bad was going to happen, right?

As I stepped off my chair en route to take a shower, my right foot came down on the side of a glass. It happened so quickly I couldn't believe how badly I cut it, but there was blood everywhere. It took an hour for the doctor to arrive, and when he got there he said, "There's nothing I can do." That gave everyone a world of confidence, though I suppose he deserved points for honesty.

Eventually, I was transported by ambulance to the next town, where they have a fairly big hospital, and by then I was getting scared. I started mentally going through the course list at the University of Wisconsin because I thought my career might be over. They put me under to do the surgery, and I can tell you there's nothing scarier than waking up in a hospital ward in the middle of the night, with a half-dozen other patients in the room, and nobody's speaking your language. I had picked up a lot of German along the way—it was probably my best subject in school—but certainly not enough to know what they were saying about my medical condition. It turned out that one of the tendons was cut all the way through and the other was sliced halfway through. Fortunately, I had been up twelve marks in the poker game, so the evening wasn't a total loss.

Actually, the German surgeon did a great job. I have a small scar and a lot of scary memories, but it didn't affect my career. I spent about six weeks in a cast, started training again, and was feeling at full strength by the end of the year—just in time to face another setback.

I had been in good shape right up through the trials for the 1987 world team, but I started to get sick right after Christmas. I had a major league fever on New Year's Day, but, young fool that I was, I left for Europe anyway. My condition kept getting worse, and I had no power to skate. In race after race, by 200 meters I'd be dead, by 500 meters I'd be literally delirious. Skaters were beating me who couldn't get within two seconds of me under normal circumstances. The absolute low point came in the final World Cup meet of the season in Holland in March. In the 1,000 I was skating against Michael Hadshieff from Austria, who is more of an "all-arounder," someone whose best distances are 1,500 meters and up. With a lap to go I was way ahead, but he just dusted me in the last lap. It was like every skater's worst nightmare—you're out there and your skates are moving, but everybody's barreling past you.

Probably the worst thing about my sickness happened after the season, when Nick, Bonnie, and I were invited to compete on a track called Medeo in the Soviet republic of Kazakhstan. Very few Americans have ever been invited there. Medeo was kind of a magic kingdom for speed skaters, sort of like that track in Oslo, Bislett Stadium, where so many world records have been set in track and field distance races. Medeo is way up in the mountains, the highest track in the world, and there's a kind of circular wind that sweeps around it. On one side the wind would be propelling you around, and on the other the flags would be just still. Partly because of the conditions, and partly because skaters just *believed* they would skate faster there, many of the fastest times in history had been registered on that track. They didn't count as official world records because they weren't sanctioned meets, but that didn't take away the thrill of skating there.

Actually, you'll have to ask Bonnie and Nick about that particular thrill. After the local doctors examined me, they determined that racing in my weakened condition would be potentially damaging to my heart because of the altitude. I was deeply disappointed, but I had to admit they were right. So I stood there and watched as Bonnie ripped off a 500 in 39.25, best ever to that point, and Nick flew to a 36.23 in the 500 and a 1:12.05 in the 1,000. At the time, the 500 was the fastest ever (I since broke it), and the 1,000 is *still* the fastest time ever recorded but, as I said, not recognized as an official world record. Much to my regret, I've never been back to Medeo and probably never will.

When I came home, I was finally diagnosed with mononucleosis. Strangely enough, it was a huge relief. Having a name to put to my troubles was vastly superior to the alternative, which was that I had simply forgotten how to skate and would have to take up a less strenuous occupation, like librarian. When I think back on that time, I realize how unusual it was and how circumstances would've been different had I been an athlete in a more mainstream sport. There is simply no way that a member of a football or baseball team would've stuck around and competed, week after week, in a weakened condition. The problem would've been diagnosed and taken care of. And I'm not blaming anyone but myself. My sport is so individual-oriented that the decision was

● *Asleep after a tough workout? No, just napping in my wagon, at one and a half years old.*

● *That's my brother Mike, at center. I'm the quarterback: a multisport talent at only five years old.*

• *Mike, eight, Jane, twelve, and me, seven (in front), in our club uniforms after a meet in West Allis.*

• *My first Olympics: 1984 in Sarajevo, with Mom, Mike (next to her), and Dad. It's a tragedy that the building we're posing in front of no longer stands.*

● *Plyometric jumps: a big part of my strength and power training.*

● *Ready and waiting to hear the gun, a sound that I will miss very much.*

● *One huge sigh of relief after a new world record in the 1,000 meters in Lillehammer.*

● *Almost too good to be true! It finally happened—on my last chance!*

● *Robin and me in a long-awaited celebration hug.*

• *Jane wasn't quite as interested as Robin and I were at my welcome-home celebration.*

largely left on my shoulders, and, believing I was invincible, that one morning I'd wake up and suddenly feel strong again, I stayed in Europe. Today, I would've come home. But that's youth.

—

Believe it or not, I was healthy through much of the 1987–88 season. I was healthy, and my sister was dying of leukemia. My mind was sometimes elsewhere, but my body was totally engaged. After I won my world title and showed Jane the medal, I wrote in the training journal I kept at the time:

> 1988 World Sprint Champion!!! Way to go, D.J.!
> Now go to Calgary and finish what you've started!
> You're the best!

Half of me said I could do it. By this time I was clearly Eric Heiden's heir as a sprinter, the first American to win a world sprint title, in fact, since Eric had done it in 1980. But half of me said I couldn't do it, that I'd rather be home with Jane. I left for the Calgary Games with mixed feelings, to say the least.

One point I must emphasize is that, had Jane been

near death when it was time for me to leave, there is no way I would've gone. But a few days after I left, her condition gradually worsened and kept getting worse. This made it extremely hard on my family. They held a big meeting to decide who would go to Calgary and who would stay home. Jane, of course, told everybody to go, including my mother. Mom was torn. She desperately wanted to stay home, but Jane kept insisting she go to Calgary. Finally, Diane met privately with Jane and said to her, "Look, you know you want Mom here. So tell her. Otherwise, she might go to Calgary because she thinks you want her to." So at last Jane told my mom to stay, and both of them were very relieved.

Eventually, Mary, Janet, and Jim and various husbands and children drove to Calgary in three vans, and my dad flew up. On February 13, the day before the 500, Jane's lungs started to fill with fluid and the situation turned grave. I remember my father coming up to me after I finished training that day and saying, "I'm needed at home. Try to hang in there." The others wanted to go home, too, but Mom decided that I needed some support up there and they stayed.

Dad arrived at O'Hare Airport in Chicago at about 11:30 P.M. and still had to drive home from there. During his flight Jane's condition had worsened and there was some thought that she was going to die before he made it. But Mom said, "No, she'll wait for her father." He got to the hospital about 2 A.M. and spent some time with her. Up in Calgary, I knew that things were bad but couldn't be sure how bad. But by this time the rest of the family knew she was going to die that day. I wrote in my journal that night:

This is it, D.J. Do it for Jane. You, and everyone else in the family.

At about 5:30 A.M. the family was called back to the hospital. The end was near, and all wanted to say their final good-byes. It was February 14, the morning of the 500-meter race. At 6:30 everyone went in, individually, and had a moment. Jane's husband made sure that Mary, Janet, and Jim were called in Calgary, and there was only a brief discussion about whether or not to tell me.

"Everyone else had their time with Jane," said Diane, "and Dan should, too." I don't think they would've ever forgiven themselves if I hadn't had my moment. I had said good-bye to Jane when I had left for Calgary one week earlier, but she had still been doing pretty well then. So it was by no means a proper good-bye.

They called me at about 6 A.M., Calgary time. There was a knock on the door, and Brian Wanek, one of my teammates, told me I had a phone call. I knew it had to be something bad—6 A.M. phone calls are rarely anything good—and I woke up Nick, who was rooming with me, and said, "It must be Jane."

I remember running down the hall to take the elevator to the basement—that's where the phone was—and I was shaking all over. I couldn't stop. It gets a little fuzzy at this point, but I think I talked to Mike first and then to my mother, who explained that Jane's blood pressure was dropping fast and that she probably wouldn't make it through the day.

"We want you to say good-bye, Dan," my mother told me. "Jane won't be able to respond, but she will be able to understand you."

I don't remember exactly what I said, but I told her I loved her and that I was going to win the race that night for her, even though I didn't believe it myself. There was not much else to say. My sister was dying and I was helpless, so far away from her. I couldn't hear a sound, not even the whir of the respirator she was hooked up to. Later, Diane and Joanne told me that they were positive Jane heard me because she breathed on her own while I was talking. I hope so. I really hope so.

My mother came on the line after that, and I asked her if I should skate.

"You know Jane would want you to, Dan," she said.

I talked to Mike again briefly. He urged me to hang in there. And then I hung up the phone in tears. I needed to see someone from my family immediately, so I got in touch with Jim. Normally, a visitor is required to have twenty-four hours' advance notice to get into the Olympic Village, but they gave me a break and Jim came over. We spent a couple of hours in the hallway of the dorm, talking and crying and remembering the good things about our sister, which wasn't hard. Jim left, and I went to breakfast with one of my teammates, Erik Henriksen. I called Jim back right after that, and he gave me the news. It was about 11 A.M.

"Jane died, D.J.," he said. "She was just too weak to make it."

I went back to that tiny little room, and Nick was in there, sharpening his skates. He just stopped when I told him, and we sat there, not knowing what to say, for minutes. Finally, he started crying, too. Like most of the skaters, he knew all my family members personally, and he was crying not only for me but also for his own memories of Jane. I got up and gave him a little hug, and that's when my conflicted feelings of skating really came out. I told Nick I had made the decision to skate, and he backed me up. But I just couldn't get it straight in my mind—and didn't until a few years later—exactly whom I was skating for. For Jane? For my family? For me? For the team?

The funny thing is, I am absolutely positive I did the right thing. I have no regrets about skating, and I would certainly make the same decision again. But I would try to be more positive about it, to turn the warm feelings I had toward Jane into something forceful and to let myself know that it was okay to compete at the same time I was grieving. But that's easy to say now. I don't think anyone confronted with this situation could deal with it rationally the first time.

The rest of the day is a blur. We had a team meeting in one of the rooms, and the guys decided to dedicate their races to Jane. That meant a lot to me, so of course I started crying again and so did a few of my teammates. After that, Nick and I went for a little jog around the Village and I remember being really startled about how quickly the news had spread. A few people even came up to me and said, "Why did they tell you? Why didn't they just let you skate?" That made no sense. I was bound to hear the news, as they had, and I certainly wanted to get it from my loved ones. And I wanted to have that last conversation with Jane.

The race was set for early evening, 5:10 P.M., prime time back in the United States, so it could be televised. I didn't do anything different in my prerace preparation, but I distinctly remember that when I got onto the ice I felt like I hadn't been on skates in six months. The best way I can describe it is "wobbly," like someone who wasn't used to skating. Thoughts raced through my head and stuck there, like giant roadblocks. *Jane is dead. Should I be here? Jane is dead. What does everyone think about me skating? Jane is dead. How hard must this be for my parents, watching me on TV and facing the prospect of what must be the absolutely worst thing in life—burying a child? Jane is dead.*

Under other circumstances, I would've felt confident. I was in excellent physical condition and was coming off a series of terrific performances. Going into the race, and without considering the emotional weight I was carrying around, the two favorites were Uwe-Jens Mey, my good friend from East Germany, and me. There were a few good Japanese skaters, too, and the usual formidable Russians. But at any rate I was definitely being counted on for a medal. The Calgary ice (we were indoors for this one, remember) was the fastest in the world—so fast, in fact, that many wondered if it was too fast. Fast ice is no problem on the straightaways, but it can be a problem in the turns, especially if a skater isn't accustomed to going that fast. I'd had trouble with the Calgary turns during a World Cup race in December, finishing tenth in one 500 and not completing the other when I couldn't hold the last inner turn. But I had skated extremely well in five days of pre-Olympic practice.

I drew the first inner turn for my race, meaning that I finished on the outside. That was the desirable draw because, as I said before, it's easier to have the final outer when you're at your highest rate of speed. If you look at clips from some 500-meter races on fast ice, in fact, you'll see guys coming out of that last inner turn going way out into the outer lane. It's almost funny to watch, unless you happen to be the skater.

The only thing I remember about being at the starting line is that I wasn't focused on the race—a fatal flaw, to say the least. To a person, my whole family, those at the Games and those watching at home, said I looked like a ghost, all the color drained from my face. My mother was absolutely convinced that she was correct to have told me to skate until she saw me at the line. "My God," she said. "What have we asked him to do?" Everything seemed to be happening as if in a dream, and I just couldn't get myself to concentrate. When I looked at the videotape later, the ABC commentator was saying, "The eyes of the world are focused on Dan Jansen," but I had no perception of what was happening to me. The best way to describe the final part of that awful tragic day is through my journal. Oddly, I have no memory of writing the entry for February 14, 1988. I must've gone back to my room after the 500 and used it as a kind of therapy. The words still bring tears to my eyes today:

> When I got to the line, I don't remember what I was thinking but I know that when the starter said "ready," I wasn't. I wasn't the same as usual, ready to blast off the line and kick everyone's butt.
>
> Then I jumped [false-started], which is rare for me.
>
> I waited on the second start and got off slow. The 100 was terrible, I was slipping, I couldn't power it like I usually do. 9.9 for me is hideous—I should've been 9.6 or 9.7.

I set the turn up OK, but in my second stroke, my left outer might as well have been on a banana peel. It just didn't hold me at all.

What a day! Good night, Jane. Rest in peace.

Only after I saw the replay of the race did I really get to analyze it. The whole thing was—and still is—a blur. I saw my false start, I saw my left skate go out from under me on the corner, I saw me knock down Yasushi Kuroiwa, I saw me hit the pads so hard that a rinkside photographer's camera fell right down beside me as I bounced back onto my feet, I saw me take off my hood and hold my head in my hands, I saw me go over and apologize to Yasushi (who got a restart and eventually finished twelfth). I saw all those things, but I don't remember any of them clearly.

What I do recall was my mixed emotions after the race. For thirty seconds I'd be sitting there and thinking, "Man, if you could've held that turn, maybe . . ." then I'd catch myself and think, "My God, you jerk, your sister just died." It was real confusing. I didn't know exactly what I was feeling or even what I *should* be feeling. I only wish I'd known Robin or Dr. Loehr at that point.

The support I received over the following days was overwhelming. Thousands of residents from the West Allis area sent me a ninety-six-foot-long signed banner with big red letters that read: DAN, BE STRONG! KEEP THE FAITH! WISCONSIN IS WITH YOU ALL THE WAY. I got flowers from the luge team, cards from the hockey team, and hang-in-theres from everyone. My parents sent Mike up to Calgary because they felt I needed him, and they were right. The newscasts were invariably sympathetic toward me, if a bit too persistent, and it was the media that later voted me the Olympic Spirit Award, which I received after the Games. It was very nice, and I appreciated it.

But from that moment forward I was unofficially ordained Dan Jansen, The Guy Who Fell on the Day His Sister Died. And Jane was known as The Sister Who Died on the Day of the Olympic 500-Meter Race. There was nothing I could've done about it, but I grew to hate those labels.

By February 18, the day of the 1,000, I was convinced I could make something positive out of these Calgary Games. Because I was not grieving on the outside, I assumed I was in good shape and could turn in a world-class 1,000. So I dedicated the race to Jane.

As I lined up for my 1,000, there seemed to be nothing standing in my way. I took the outside lane next to Guy Thibault of Canada and got off quickly. *Do it for Jane.* At 200 meters I was leading the field, at 400 meters I was leading the field, at 600 meters I was leading the field, at 800 meters . . . I was down. I fell on a straightaway, catching an outer edge. Mike was watching the race up in the stands, and right before that he turned to his wife, Angie, and said, "Dan's got it made now. He's made it through the toughest turns." Gradually, the family learned. In the Olympics, Dan *never* has it made.

"Catching an outer" means exactly what it sounds like—you roll too far over on the outer edge of your skate, and that causes you to fall. It's closer to an act of God than a mistake, and every skater has done it at least once. Catching an outer at the Olympics, though, was a triumph of timing of which only Dan Jansen was capable. Why did it happen? Why then?

I know why now. I know I just could not bring myself to win. It wasn't right, it wasn't just, that I should win a medal when my sister was not yet buried.

Somebody asked Pete, then the West German coach, about my race. "That wasn't Dan Jansen skating," Pete said. "That was his body, but it wasn't him. That man was in shock. I don't think he knew it himself." As usual, Pete knew best.

Right after the 1,000 I flew home in a private jet with Mike, Jim, and Janet. I remember we were listening to music and a song by Alabama came on that included the lyric "I'm falling again." So I started singing it to myself, softly at first, then a little louder. "I'm falling again." "I'm falling again." Pretty soon we all started laughing.

From time to time over the next few years, I remembered that moment. But I had a hard time conjuring up much laughter.

CHAPTER 5

Lillehammer

It would be nice to report that my mental condition for the 1,000-meter race on the eighteenth improved steadily day by day, thus proving that I was a completely balanced, healthy individual who had shrugged off the baggage of the past and was looking forward to my final Olympic challenge.

Sounds good, right?

It didn't happen that way. For whatever reason, I woke up on this day with a terrible mental attitude, much worse than the day before, when logic says I should've been down. But logic has nothing to do, I discovered, with the average athlete's psyche.

When I went to the rink, I couldn't shake the feeling that everyone was talking about me and feeling sorry for me. And of all the emotions you can stir in people, pity is the worst. Perhaps I was imagining it, but as someone once said, "Just because I'm paranoid doesn't mean no one's chasing me."

I was tired of being the object of pity, the brave guy in the face of adversity. My father told a reporter, "We're as proud of Dan for the way he handled defeat as for all the victories he's had." Dad meant every word, but the point is, I was sick to death of handling defeat in a grand fashion. What I wanted and needed was a chance to handle victory with humility. Let's try that in an Olympic setting just once.

I sat on the bench for the longest time. "I just don't feel like skating today," I told Pete. And he would say, "I know, D.J., just hang in there. It'll pass. It really will." I wasn't in the dumps just because of my slip in the 500 two days earlier. It was more a collective feeling of failure, all the devastating experiences of 1988 in Calgary and 1992 in Albertville coming down on me. I had truly believed before the Lillehammer Games that the 500-meter race was going to bring an end to my misery. I felt strong and confident. And though my family didn't tell me this until later, they felt the same way. And when it didn't happen, the thought started creeping into my mind that it just wasn't going to happen.

But as the day wore on and I started to work out, the negative feelings were pushed aside. One thing my work with Dr. Loehr had accomplished was to teach me not to stay down too long. You can go down, D.J., he'd tell me, but just make sure you come back up. And when I came back up on this day, one overwhelming thought came into my mind:

How many golfers blow a winning putt at the Masters and get another chance to make it? How many basketball players blow a big free throw in the NCAA finals and get another chance to sink one the next year? Not many. I was truly blessed to be getting a final opportunity. It wasn't all luck. The major reason I was getting another shot was because I'd hung in there, trained hard, and remained at the top of my sport. But though negative circumstances had conspired to deny me a medal in 1988 and '92, a set of positive circumstances had again dumped me at fortune's doorstep in 1994. And I was glad to be there.

I thought of the hundreds and hundreds of other athletes I had known over the years who never got their shot at glory, athletes who'd duckwalked those same hills and ridden that same stationary bike for hours but never got the real payoff. And a few of them were close to me, men whose strength, determination, and support had been—and would be again in the upcoming 1,000—important factors in my success. Words really can't express what Andy Gabel, Nick Thometz, and Mike Jansen have meant to me as a human being and as a skater. But I'll give it a try. And it's as good a time as any to talk about the special relationship I've had with a skater who *is* known—Bonnie Blair.

—

A psychologist would say—as a matter of fact, Dr. Loehr *has* said—that Andy Gabel ("Gabes" to everyone in the speed-skating community) is my flip side, the heads to my tails, the yin to my yang. It's true to a certain extent but, like most generalizations, only to an extent. Andy is probably a lot more serious than he seems, particularly about skating, and at times, when I'm away from the ice, I can be as open and carefree as Andy. Over the years, in fact, I think some of Andy has rubbed off on me and some of me has rubbed off on Andy. It could hardly have been otherwise. For the better part of twenty years we've been competitors and training partners, roommates and golfing buddies. We've laughed and cried and leaned on each other during the hard times.

After competing against me as a junior, Andy gradually discovered that short-track skating was more to his liking, and, indeed, he seems to have the classic personality for it—outgoing, explosive, speaks his mind, holds nothing back. If speed skaters like myself are anonymous most of the time, short-trackers are practically invisible *all* the time. It kind of surprises me that Andy's sport doesn't get more coverage during the Olympics, but to the television people it seems to be about as popular as the biathlon. So nobody knows that Gabes has been one of the best short-trackers in the world over the last six years.

As I said before, Olympic heartbreak didn't begin and end with me. Gabes's bad luck and disappointment were just as profound as my own, even if no one was

chronicling it for posterity. He had completely dominated the 500 meters in his sport during the 1993–94
season, much as I had the 500 in long track, and going
into Lillehammer he was a clear favorite, probably for
the gold but certainly for a medal. Like me, various circumstances had kept him from getting one in either '88
or '92.

Anyway, during his 500-meter race he was just flat
knocked down by a Chinese skater, the kind of reckless
incident that only happens in the Olympics when short
track suddenly turns into a demolition derby. After a
long conference the officials decided to disqualify the
Chinese skater but not to advance Gabes, a clear viola-
tion not only of the rules but also of logic. Gone was his
chance for a gold medal. And in an incredible case of
bad timing, his relay race was scheduled two hours after
the 500. I was there to comfort him, just as he had been
there to comfort me after many of my disappointments.

"Gabes, you're the captain of this team and you're
never going to win a medal unless you're at your best
and pumpin'," I told him. We were over at the rink
playing hackeysack and just talking. He was as far down
as I've ever seen him. "It's up to you, Gabes," I told
him. "You're the leader. You set the pace." I sounded

like Dr. Loehr. And, slowly but surely, Andy pulled out of it. I'm not sure I could've done the same, but he went out and fired off several excellent legs and the U.S. team ended up with a silver, which was a great showing. And though very few people outside the sport know his name, Andy Gabel's silver medal took just as much work and determination as my gold.

Nick Thometz, on the other hand, is the best skater *never* to have won an Olympic medal. I'm absolutely convinced of that. You think I've had bad luck? Nick was right there in the front of the line when those two words were invented.

How good was he? Well, I already told you about his performances at Medeo. And going into the '88 Olympic year, when I fully intended to win a medal, our coach at the time, Mike Crowe, told the press that America's two best hopes for a medal were Bonnie Blair and Nick Thometz. He was probably correct. Nick is small for a sprinter, a shade under 5'9" and about 160 pounds, but it never mattered because he was—and still is—an absolutely brilliant technical skater. And whatever Gabes did for my head, psyching me up when I was down, Nick did for my technical proficiency on the ice.

From 1981, the year when we were first on the national team together, Nick and I were training partners. It seems like we've skated together a million times, first him in front, then me in front, replicating each other's long, smooth strokes, concentrating on gliding rather than running. It was hard, painful work that, to say the least, was best done with someone else. Nick and I were similar personalities, guys who were serious on the ice, never afraid of hard work, and fairly quiet off it. Had we resembled each other more physically, we would've been nearly mirror images in competition.

Yet, oddly, we never seemed to skate at top form together. When I was sick or injured, Nick was skating great; when I was skating great, Nick was sick or injured. As I look back on my career, one of the few regrets I have is that there was never an Olympic Games when Nick and I were able to go for the gold, man against man, without a hundred extenuating circumstances. It would've been beautiful.

But it didn't happen that way. In one of those peculiarly cruel episodes of timing that seem to follow me around, Nick's career took a nosedive on the same weekend—the trials for the 1988 Olympic team in early December of 1987—that Jane came out of remission and had to be readmitted to the hospital. That's when

Nick learned he had a blood disorder called ITP. (I won't attempt to give you the official medical term for the disease, which Nick can rattle off as easily as a lap time.) Strangely, ITP is somewhat similar to leukemia though infinitely more controllable. Basically, the disease causes Nick to have chronic low platelets (platelets are necessary for proper clotting), in his case because they are eaten up when they pass through the spleen.

The disease made him tired, and gradually it started to have an effect on his skating. This point has been made before, but in a sport where hundredths of a second are crucial, one can imagine how devastating this disease would be. No matter how hard he trained—and no one trained harder—Nick couldn't overcome his feelings of fatigue. For a very short time he took a corticosteroid intended to control his ITP, but this type of steroid (unlike anabolic steroids) weakens the body rather than strengthening it. Nick quickly chose to do without this medication altogether. Although he would fight his condition bravely, eventually it ended his competitive career.

Going into the Calgary Games, only those closest to him knew about the disease and even we didn't fully understand it, so he was still considered one of the favorites in both the 500 and 1,000. But in his own way, Nick was as doomed physically as I was mentally. He was sort of my polar opposite. He felt fine on top but his body let him down, whereas my body felt fine but my head wasn't in it. He finished eighth in the 500 and eighteenth in the 1,000. Nick could still put together some good races from time to time simply because he was so talented. As late as 1990, in the U.S. sprint championships in Butte, Montana, he set a track record of 37.19 in the 500 meters. But no matter how hard he tried, he just couldn't beat the ITP. In Albertville in '92, he was thirteenth in the 500 and fifteenth in the 1,000. By the next year, his career was over. His disease is not life-threatening, but it kept him from being recognized as a true great in the sport.

For four straight years Nick Thometz finished fourth in the World Cup, just out of the medals. He missed a bronze in the 1,000 in Sarajevo, when he was just a kid, by one tenth of a second. And just as he seemed to be coming into his own, he found out about ITP. Yet whatever I went through, there was Nick right beside me, cheering me on, lifting me up. He did it in a quieter fashion than Gabes did, but he was just as sincere. Don't shed any tears for Nick Thometz, because he doesn't want them any more than I do. But if you ever feel a moment's sadness for what I went through, give a moment to Nick, too. He deserves it.

And I thought, too, of Bonnie, of how unique and special it was that a man and a woman had the chance to work so closely together as athletes and friends. If I knew one thing, I knew that Bonnie, in my position, wouldn't have backed down from the challenge, no matter how formidable it might've been.

Bonnie and I go back a long way, as far back as I go with Nick and Gabes and J.B. I remember having a crush on her when I was about nine years old, but more important, through the years we've been buddies, training mates, and each other's cheerleaders. We never, ever turned our relationship into a Billie Jean King–Bobby Riggs type of thing. Bonnie was a woman competing against women—and in my mind she's the best female sprinter who ever lived—and I was a man competing against men. We skated against each other in a fun 500-meter race for charity a few years back; Bonnie got a three-second head start and we finished almost in a dead heat. And three seconds has more or less remained the magic difference between us.

But we don't think about that. The important thing is that we've been able to help each other. She's benefited from skating in my (and Nick's) strides, and that has helped her establish power on her glides. Also, when she's behind us, she can draft off us so she can *feel* that speed, accustom herself to it, which a lot of women who don't train with men can't do. From Bonnie I've gained a real sense of technique on turns, because she is unquestionably one of the most technically proficient skaters *ever*. Also, Bonnie has helped me out a lot over the years, because I'll go out and watch her race and, based on her time, get a pretty good idea of the conditions. Then, too, Bonnie has snapped me awake more than once during a race because of her voice, which is rather distinctive, like my sister Diane's. I'd be skating along, blocking out everything, and all of a sudden I'd hear Bonnie, above the crowd, urging me to get going.

The thing that has impressed me most about Bonnie is her dedication. I'm not exactly known as a party animal, but Bonnie . . . well, let's just say there were lots of times when we wanted Bonnie to ease up a little and have some more fun. But what Bonnie has done is serve as a strong example to the younger generation of skaters, many of whom would otherwise think the most important aspect of training in Europe is learning to drink exotic brands of beer.

There was never, ever any jealousy between us. If anything, perhaps I felt a little guilty about getting some of the recognition I did for failing in the Olympics, while Bonnie was getting the same—and maybe a little less—for winning. But she understood, more than anyone, what I accomplished in the off-Olympic years and how the attention was justified.

As I regained my motivation that day, I could feel Bonnie with me, pushing me, hollering at me to get going. She knew better than almost anyone around me what I had gone through. And I didn't want to let her down.

The final key to my coming out of a funk that day was thinking about my brother, whose story in some ways parallels both Andy's and Nick's. Mike's nickname in the skating community was (and still is) Woody, for a particularly ridiculous reason. One day years and years ago he was skating around the track with one of our friends who was a *Saturday Night Live* freak. The night before, Bill Murray had done his drama-critic bit, in which he'd kept referring to Woody Allen as "Woodman." Mike was a big fan of the show, too, and every time this guy would skate by he'd say, "Hey, Woody. The Woodman." Next thing you know, Mike was Woody; maybe he just seemed like a Woody.

My mother used to say that Mike and I might as well have been twins because we were so close. I have an excellent relationship with my parents, but I've never really confided in them for the simple reason that I always had Jane on the one side and Mike on the other. I think my mother came to understand that.

No one has stood behind me more steadfastly than Mike, and I often wonder if I would've had the strength of character to do that if our situations had been reversed. Remember that he, not I, was the big brother, the one who had all the success first. Nick tells the story of going against Mike when they were about eleven years old. He looked over at my brother and thought to himself, "Man, this kid could be shaving." I remember registering for a junior meet in New York one year and the lady who signed me in said, "Oh, you're the Jansen boy we've heard so much about." And I just smiled and said thank you, but I was *not* the Jansen boy they heard so much about. I told Mike and my family about it, and we all got a laugh. Mike became the North American champion in that meet, while I only finished fourth in my division. My mother talks about how she used to overhear all the side betting that went on at meets, and she says that most of the money was usually on Mike.

In a way, our situation in athletics was foreshadowed within the family by both Mary and Janet and Jim and Dick. Mary was older than Janet but had to grin and bear it when Janet started beating her. Jim was older than Dick but never could beat him because Dick was such a superior athlete. And both of the older kids will concede that it was tough on them. But Mike, even though our competition was played out on a much larger and much more public stage, seemed to be completely comfortable with it.

As I said before, our paths probably began to diverge in high school, when I decided to give up football to concentrate on skating and Mike kept on playing. He came back to skating after his senior year, but—who knows?—maybe that little bit of an edge I had gained put me ahead of him permanently. Mike doesn't think so. He is comfortable with the fact that he was never a superb technician and believes he went as far as he could have gone. Pete is convinced, on the other hand, that with a stronger commitment to conditioning Mike would've been more of a factor in the world speed-skating picture. But as it was, Mike didn't do badly. His main problem was carrying around the Jansen knack for bad luck and awful timing.

Mike missed making the 1984 Olympic team in the 1,000 by seventeen hundredths of a second. And two false starts may have kept him from qualifying in the 500. In '88, when in my opinion he was the third best 500 man in the United States, behind Nick and me, he pulled a groin muscle a week before the trials. Later on, he wondered if it had happened because he was supposed to stay home with Jane and that only one Jansen brother was destined to be in Calgary. I wonder, too. He came back again for '92, but the groin continued to bother him and he had fallen too far behind. His career was over, and today the vast majority of people don't even remember how great a skater he was.

I don't know how Mike handled my success so easily. I used to think about it from time to time and wonder if he resented me. But I became convinced over the years that he was never anything less than honest, that he felt as good for me as he seemed to. My mother once said that Mike accepted losing better than I did and perhaps that kept him from the top. But in his own way, Mike handled pressure and disappointment every bit as well as I did.

When I got back to my room on this day, feeling a little bit better about my chances, there was a fax waiting for me. It said: "Obviously, things didn't go the way you wanted in the 500. But you have family and friends back home who still love you and care about you. And more importantly you have a 1,000-meter race to get up for, so go out and kick ass!" Woody Jansen sent that fax, and he'll never know how much it meant to me.

INTERLUDE V

We buried Jane on a typically cold, gray Wisconsin afternoon, February 21, 1988. People waited in line for two hours to pay their final respects at our church, St. Augustine. Some were there, I suppose, because of the publicity her death had generated from Calgary, but not many. Most of them knew someone in the Jansen family, probably my father, and therefore by extension all of us. My brothers and sisters and I used to joke that we couldn't go anywhere in West Allis without twenty-five people saying hello to Dad, that he might as well have been mayor of the town. It was a peculiar experience for me. I was away from home so often that I didn't see my old friends as much as I would've liked, and suddenly there they were, and on such a sad occasion. There were dozens and dozens of policemen and firemen in uniform at the church, the former group because of the Jansen family, the latter because of Jane's husband, Rich.

It was a difficult time for everyone. Monsignor Francis Beres, Rich's uncle, gave the homily. He did a great job, but his voice finally cracked at the end when he said: "So, Jane, as we bid you farewell we ask God to shower on us strength and courage and perseverance." Father John Yockey, who's a professor of theology from Washington and the brother of Janet's husband, Don, brought up the Olympics in his tribute. Somebody wrote down the words for me:

"Dan, you loved Jane as profoundly as she loved you. She told you to go for it and you did and we are so proud of you, just as Jane is. You have taught us one of the most important lessons in life. You see, we all fall. Sometimes early on and sometimes when things are coming together. But we thank you for showing us how to get up again with dignity and love and to stay together with your family and friends and to see it through to the finish line. You come from a family of champions. You are a champion, just like Jane is, and all of us are privileged to be your friends. So we will pull together and stay together and love because Jane is with us and cheering us on. We, too, will continue the race until we finish the race."

I was doing pretty well at the funeral until Father Yockey said those words, and then I just lost it. But that's okay. Funerals are not for holding in emotions. They're for remembering your loved ones in a personal and emotional way. Soon after that they played "On Eagles' Wings," Jane's favorite hymn, and that was very, very hard for all of us. I doubt if any Jansen has ever heard that hymn since without shedding a tear.

Pull together. Stay together. Whatever bad moments came out of Jane's death—and there were many—I never doubted that the one advantage our family would have is that we would pull together and stay together. I really feel for people who don't have that kind of love and support when a loved one is lost. I don't know how anyone can get through that alone.

The question everyone asks themselves, of course, is:

Why? Why put two good people like Harry and Gerry Jansen through the pain of losing a child, the absolute worst human tragedy? Why emotionally punish a good person like Joanne, who, to this day, still has trouble dealing with Jane's death? And why, in a family with four strong, healthy male siblings, was Jane the one chosen to suffer? Not a day went by during that terrible period when Jim, Dick, Mike, or I did not say to ourselves, "Why couldn't it have been one of us instead of Jane?" To ask such questions is not, I think, a rejection of one's faith. And if it is, well, I'm sorry. Ultimately, I think all of us came to grips with the fact that there are mysteries we don't understand and that maybe, someday, we'll get the chance to be with Jane again.

The one thing I often wonder about—and I never talked to her about it because I just couldn't find the right moment—is whether or not Jane was afraid to die. She always seemed so calm and composed. As I said, her strength of character compelled her to fight the disease for a year, but in those final days, when she finally knew it would beat her, did she get frightened? Did she feel incomplete? Or, as Jim thought, was it enough for her to have given birth to three beautiful daughters and made lots of people happy along the way? Some people say it would be the most awful thing in the world to know when you are going to die, but others believe it's a blessing, that knowing enables you to plan the things you want to do. All things considered, I think I would rather not know. But when my time comes, I hope I can meet it with the strength of character Jane showed.

My memories of that day are, of course, sad and depressing. But the only thing that I would call "negative" happened when I was walking out of the church and saw photographers in the balcony. I wasn't expecting it because I had been told that the press would not be allowed in. They were actually reasonable and didn't try to interview me or the family. Over the years an athlete has to come to terms with the press and the fact that, if they celebrate you during the good times, then you must expect they will cover you during the bad ones as well. I've accepted that. Up in Calgary a few of my teammates had gotten mad at the media for their constant coverage of my two falls, but I tried to understand. In fact, after most of my disappointments at the Olympics, I usually wanted to talk, maybe just to let people know I was all right, that life would go on. But I couldn't help feeling angry on this day because I knew none of the photographers would've been there if not for the connection to the Olympics.

If someone asks me about Jane now, I'm usually willing to talk about her. The more we talk about her, the more people will remember her as an individual, rather than just as part of my story. But it's never easy and it's never unemotional. I remember someone asking my father once—this was about four or five years after she died—if talking about his daughter had gotten easier over the years.

"Well," he said. "I don't cry every time I mention her name, if that's what you mean."

That's how we all feel.

In the weeks following the Olympics I received between 7,000 and 8,000 letters from all over the world, and it would be silly to pretend that many of them were not the result of Jane. I wish it were otherwise, that they would've been recognizing me as an athlete and Jane as a living, breathing person, but it didn't happen that way. I will say that none of the letters seemed like a fake, that all of the people who took the time were honestly affected by the story. I guess the most moving note I got was from a thirty-year-old man from Doylestown, Pennsylvania, who had won a gold medal in the Special

Olympics, the competition for physically and mentally challenged individuals. He actually sent me the medal he won. Here's what he wrote:

Dear Dan,

I watched you on TV. I'm sorry that you fell 2 times. I am in Special Olympics. I won a gold medal at the Pa. State Summer Olympics right after my Dad died seven years ago. Before we start the Games we have a saying that goes like this. Let me win but if I can't win let me be brave in the attempt.

I want to share one of my gold medals with you because I don't like to see you not get one. Try again in four more years.

The man's name was Mark Arrowood. We eventually struck up a relationship, and I even visited him once. Sadly, he died a few years later. How many hundreds and hundreds of stories of courage and determination, like Mark's, will never be known?

—

I returned to Calgary the day after the funeral. A number of my friends still had to compete, Bonnie and Andy among them, and my girlfriend at the time, Natalie Grenier, a speed skater from Canada, hadn't raced yet. I wanted to be there to support them. Natalie skated very well in her all-around events but didn't win a medal— she was never one of the world's elite. But Bonnie broke through and won the gold in the 500, which was something of a surprise. The East Germans, most of whom were on steroids, as they later admitted, were dominant at that time, and Bonnie had been trying for years to get past them. She finally did, and everyone in the American skating community was proud of her.

I suspect many people figured I shriveled up and disappeared after Calgary. Quite the opposite happened, in fact. I won a World Cup 500-meter sprint race in Savalen, Norway, on March 5, just three weeks after my Olympic races, and Nick (third) and I (second) both medaled in the 1,000. And a week later I won the 1,000 in a World Cup event in Inzell, West Germany. But I'm not going to pretend everything was normal. First of all, there's a natural letdown for every Olympic athlete after the Games, never mind the additional burdens I was carrying. My brother Mike told me later that I seemed to walk around in a daze for weeks after the Games and really didn't come to grips with everything for a long while. In one sense, I suppose, I really didn't come to grips with it until a few *years* later, after I started working with Dr. Loehr. I do know that those months immediately following Calgary represented the hardest extended period of my life.

As I said before, the vast majority of people couldn't have been kinder or had better intentions in dealing with the Jansen family tragedy. But there were a select few who made it tough. There was one radio station that had a continuing gag about the towns around Milwaukee named Falls, such as Black River Falls and Menomonee Falls. Perhaps West Allis should change its name to Jansen Falls, went the joke. I'm telling you, that one had me rollin' in the aisles. And then there was the night when Woody, Rick Smith, and I came through the door of a restaurant, and a woman looked at me and said, "Don't trip, now." Mike had to be talked out of beating up the woman's boyfriend as his show of dissatisfaction with the quip.

Comments like those never really upset me, despite the fact that I admit to being much more sensitive than I appear. My explanation is that certain people, like that woman, are so ignorant that they don't deserve my anger. Anyway, I'm not a fighting man. Outside of trading a few blows with my brothers from time to time, I've never been in a real fight. And I could just picture the headline if I had taken the bait: OLYMPIC LOSER HAS RABBIT EARS, PUNCHES OUT FAN IN BAR.

The internal sadness I was feeling, though, went beyond the outward events of Jane's death and my two falls. The timing of those two things led me to examine whether my life was really going in the right direction. And my relationship with Natalie was not going well, even though we had been discussing marriage. I was planning to take some time away from skating and attend classes at the University of Calgary, where I would be near her. I didn't know whether it was a mistake or not. The '92 Olympics were a long way off, and I wondered if I could stay on top for that long. Many of the kids I had gone to school with were graduating from college and starting careers. What was I doing?

So it was with some trepidation that I became a part-time student in Calgary. I had trigonometry, an English course, and a French course. I had learned a lot of the language from traveling and being around Natalie, but, predictably, I was weak on the grammar.

But before I started the semester, the most wonderful thing happened. Wonderful and wonderfully confusing at the same time. I met Robin.

It happened in August. Maxwell House, which sponsored the Olympic Spirit Award, asked me, as the winner of the award, to make an appearance in Charlotte, North Carolina, to help open the new Charlotte Coliseum. Those kinds of affairs were always fun and I was glad to do them, but to say they were anything special would be an exaggeration. Anyway, I met a guy named Mark Richardson, whose father, Jerry, an ex–NFL player, was the moving force behind the Carolina Panthers, which at the time were bidding (successfully, as it turned out) to become an NFL expansion team. Mark was engaged to Joan Wicker (they later married), Joan being the younger sister of a woman named Robin Wicker.

Mark asked me to go out with him and some friends after the ceremony, and for the life of me I don't know why I said yes. Generally I get asked to go out after my official duties are done and generally I say no, but on this night I said yes. And after I did, Mark introduced me to another person who just happened to be along. That was Robin.

Mark has always been a little hazy on this point, but the evidence points to the fact that he had something in mind from the beginning. At the time Robin was involved in a relationship with a guy named Eric Eichmann, who was a national-class soccer player. Robin says she would not have gone out with us all had she known Mark had matchmaking on his agenda, and I wouldn't have either. As soon as we arrived at the restaurant, Robin called Eric and told him where she was. Of course, she neglected to mention that I was along.

Well, we talked and talked that night, and a whole new world opened up for me. And when I mention how easily things went with Robin from the beginning, it's not a slight on Natalie. Natalie is a wonderful person, but the way I saw it, the relationship was not growing. I know she disagrees. One of the difficult things about the situation was that I didn't have one firm reason why I wanted to break up. I couldn't say, "You did this," or "I hated this." I know the whole thing has been tougher on her because Robin and I are so happy. I'm sorry about that, but it was better that the breakup happened when it did.

Perhaps it was inevitable. There are many athletes within my sport who have relationships, so I'm not going to proclaim that it doesn't work. But it can be a problem when the man and the woman do the same thing. You don't get an outside perspective, and the whole relationship becomes so insular. You're either training, talking about training, thinking about train-ing, hearing somebody else talking about training, com-peting, or thinking about competing.

I'm just saying that for me to hear another under-standing voice opened up a whole new world. I could be very open with Robin, and she seemed to understand what I needed to hear. She wasn't familiar with me, out-side of knowing I was the poor unfortunate who had fallen twice in Calgary, and Lord knows she wasn't a skating fan. The first time she got onto on skates, which was after she met me, she had to crawl around the rink with both hands on the railing.

That night I fell and fell hard. And I wasn't even on ice.

Robin was a little more wary. When I called her the next morning and asked to see her that night, she hesi-tated. She later admitted to having had a "bad case of the guilts," but she finally said yes. We attended another Coliseum function and had to pretend we really weren't there "together." Those kinds of situations are hysteri-cal in sitcoms but not nearly so funny in real life. I left Charlotte the next day and put this message on her an-swering machine at work: "I left something in Char-lotte. I'll be back to get it."

The next few months were very hard. Robin and I are not the first people to have been in this situation, and we certainly won't be the last, but that was little compensation for the mixed emotions we were feeling. Both of us had to break off long-term relationships with people we cared about; I'm not the type who is good at hurting other people's feelings, and neither is Robin. Besides, being monogamous is a way of life in our family. Even when I had a girlfriend at an early age, I was always loyal to her.

We also had to figure out a way to see if our relationship could grow even though we were a thousand miles apart. From the time we met, in August 1988, until we got married in April 1990, we probably spent only three or four months together. We also had to straighten out our professional lives; Robin had a good job with Marriott Hotels and had to figure out where she wanted to go with that, and I had to start refocusing on skating for the 1989 season. And all this was swirling around in my head while the sad memories of Calgary and Jane's death were still prominent.

We talked and talked and talked some more—about Jane, about the Olympics, about our relationship, and about what we wanted our future relationship to be.

Strange thoughts, fragments of memories from those terrible days in Calgary, things I had blocked out, would all of a sudden come rushing back to me, and I'd need to talk to Robin about them. My phone bill was $800 one month, mostly on phone calls from Calgary to Charlotte. I've made the point that I always did have a great support system, both within my family and from people like Gabes and J.B. and Nick. But by this time in my life I needed someone with an outside perspective, someone who didn't know every detail of my life. That's what Robin brought.

There were obstacles, but finally we just decided to step over them or barrel our way through them. I wanted to be with Robin, and that was that. In the summer of 1989 I was up at the family cottage on Long Lake, about an hour north of West Allis, with J.B. and Gabes and Woody, and I told them I was thinking about popping the question. They had one unified response: "Go for it!" So I went for it. Robin was coming to visit on July 4, and I decided that would be a good time. That night we went to a restaurant on the lake-front. After we ordered our food, I demonstrated my knack for clear speech and lucid communication.

"You know how we always talk about the future and getting married someday and all that?" I said.

Robin said, "Yes."

I said, "Well, you know, I'd like to do it pretty soon."

Robin said, "Yes."

I said, "Well, will you marry me?"

She said, "Yes, sure, I guess so."

She thought it was just more vague talk about the future, so I said, "No, you don't understand. I mean, I want to do it now. This is a proposal."

And then she couldn't eat. I mean, I really took her by surprise. She got up from the table and disappeared for twenty minutes. I just asked the woman to spend the rest of her life with me and she's gone. It turned out she had called her family back home and was telling everybody the news.

I took that as a yes.

Robin comes from a family that's in some ways similar to mine and in others completely different. The main distinction is that the Jansens are Midwest and the Wickers are South. You could devote a whole book to those differences, so I won't even get into it. But her family is as close as mine and wanted the best for Robin as much as my family wanted the best for me. Fortunately, they accepted me from the beginning, and that made a big, big difference.

We got married nine months later, in April 1990, in a big southern-style wedding in Newberry, South Carolina, Robin's hometown. You can guess my wedding party. Woody was best man, and Gabes, Nick, J.B., and Rick Smith were the groomsmen. I brought the Jansen luck with me to the wedding weekend. It rained so hard in the morning that we had to cancel the outside reception we had planned after the ceremony.

But it didn't matter. We were married, and I was glad. I'm still glad.

To some people we might look like an odd mix—the outgoing woman from the South and the taciturn man from the Midwest—but I think those differences turned us into a team. Robin has a good way with people, a knack for making them feel right at home. I don't have that. In fact, as I discovered later, for the longest time many of my competitors thought I was stuck up because I rarely approached people. That hurt a lot. Though I've improved in the public relations area, I still do not, as a rule, go up to people I don't know and give them a "How's it going?" I think a lot of that comes from my father. In some sense I guess Robin and I parallel my parents. When we're together, Robin tends to do most of the talking, just as my mother does. But some people misconstrue that as one person dominating the relationship. It's not like that. Robin always says I'm the one person who can put her in her place with a few words. I'm not really sure that's true, but I'll take her word for it.

Any relationship requires adjustments on both sides, but I think that's doubly true when one begins a new life with an athlete. Robin understood there was a commitment, of course, but no one can know precisely what that means until they see it firsthand. I mean, it's just not normal for your husband to come home from work and literally fall on the floor from exhaustion. And sometimes when Robin came to my workouts, she'd watch us leaping upstairs on one leg and doing other strange types of training exercises and she'd get almost frightened.

One of the most surprising things was that Robin not only agreed to but also *wanted* to live in Wisconsin. Tell you the truth, I'm still amazed by it. She had to leave her roots, give up her career, and separate herself from Renee, her twin sister, who is literally a part of her. Part of Robin's personality, though, is being able to adjust to new situations. I know she appreciates the fact that there is very little of the keeping-up-with-the-Joneses mentality in Milwaukee, as there is in Charlotte, where she was living. And though Milwaukee doesn't bear a lot of resemblance to the South, I think the family-oriented lifestyle, with Jansens here, there, and everywhere, reminded her of her own close-knit hometown.

—

Though very few people were actually paying attention, my skating continued to improve between the Olympics of 1988 and 1992. Then, too, my mental state improved under Dr. Loehr, my on-the-ice strength improved under Pete Mueller, and my personal life improved under Robin. In retrospect, however, I know that my "I love the 1,000" lessons had not fully kicked in for the Albertville Games. I was either the best or the second best 500-meter skater in the world. Everybody knew it, just as I knew it. But I simply was not prepared to accept the premise that I was also among the top two in the 1,000. And therefore I wasn't.

As had been the case in Calgary, I came into the '92

Olympics in Albertville on a strong note. In December 1991, several weeks before the Games, I skated the best 500-meter race of my life to that point. It came in the Olympic trials in West Allis, when I clocked 36.59, just fourteen hundredths of a second off Uwe-Jens Mey's world record. Then, on January 25, at a World Cup meet in Davos, Switzerland, I skated 36.41 to beat by two hundredths of a second another world record that Uwe had set just six days earlier. Going into Albertville, my German friend and I were clearly 1–2 in the 500. We had raced seven times during the season, with four wins for Uwe, two for me, and one tie. The difference in our combined time in all those races was about one fifth of a second in Uwe's favor. Is this a crazy sport or what?

But things started to go wrong after that world record. We decided to cut back on our training to be fresh for the Games, but maybe we cut back too much. The ideal strategy would've been to spend some time in In-zell, Germany, to work out, but we couldn't get onto the ice there because of the "Motorcycles on Ice" competition, which is just what it sounds like. It was too early for us to get our accommodations in Albertville, so we ended up whiling away the time in Collalbo, a small town in Italy that had nothing in particular to offer a dozen anxious speed skaters. It was nobody's fault, but I think we were a little stale coming in.

My prerace warm-ups went well, but on the morning of the 500-meter race, February 15, 1992, it started to rain. There had already been complaints about the Olympic Oval ice, which was a portable track brought in that was never used again. It was unevenly refrigerated—most portable tracks are—and there was even mud washing down on the track. One national team coach publicly called it "crap." I wasn't going to offend the Olympic organizers by seconding that notion, but it was probably true. At any rate, they should not have held the most important race in the world on such a surface. Then, too, the way they had constructed the stadium, with one side in bright sunshine and the other completely in shade, was distracting.

The rain made an already bad situation that much worse. Rain makes the ice soft and pebbly, and under those conditions your blades don't want to turn but, rather, go straight. It's bad for everybody but worse for a long, "glide" skater like me. Yet I couldn't suddenly become a "runner," taking short, choppy steps, like the

Japanese skaters, after years and years of doing it my way.

Nick Thometz was in the first pair, and I was anxious to see how he would do to get some kind of clue about the ice. It was rainy and the temperature was about 50°F., ideal for a marathon but not for the Olympic 500-meter speed-skating event. Nick's time was 37.83, which was not bad considering that he was still battling his ailment and hadn't been much of a force before the Games. But I knew I would have to go faster.

I was in the second pair and felt fairly confident. At least, I thought I did. Robin had made me a sweatshirt that said: "Carpe Diem, D.J." But instead the day seized me. I skated a race that I can only describe as perfect but tentative. I didn't slip. I looked good. The race looked fine on replay. But something kept me from really going after it, from flat out *overpowering* the race, like I do when I'm really in form. That's the only way I can describe what happened. When I crossed the finish line, I really didn't have to look at my time, which was 37.46, because I knew it wouldn't be good enough for a gold and perhaps not even for a medal. Nick later told the press: "When Dan crossed the line, he seemed more confused than anything. I don't know if he really knew what had happened."

That's accurate, I suppose. Even under those conditions, I believed I could've skated under 37, and, tell you the truth, I'm not quite sure why it didn't happen. Maybe deep down, I needed just to stay up in an Olympic race after the two falls in '88. I've heard people say that and I never really subscribed to it, but it seems to be as good as any theory I've got.

However, Dr. Loehr, who's more capable of finding a psychological aspect than anyone, feels that I was absolutely prepared to win the race and that it came down to the technical problem with the ice. Okay, I'm willing to consider that, too. But I do know that part of the beauty of sports is its unpredictability. And of my eight Olympic races, two each in '84, '88, '92, and '94, the 500 in Albertville remains the most mysterious and frustrating.

The results didn't help me analyze it any more clearly, either. Uwe won the gold in 37.14, a relatively slow time. He's a power skater, too, so obviously he adjusted better than I did. But the fact that a prime-timer like him won the race also indicates that it could've been a psychological barrier, that the opportunity was there for me to win but I just wasn't prepared to seize it. Two

Japanese skaters, Toshiyuki Kuroiwa and Junichi Inoue, took silver and bronze in 37.18 and 37.26, which tells me that ice conditions had a lot to do with the results. Junichi was a complete unknown at the time but was able to master the conditions because of his shorter, choppier style.

And who finished fourth, the place that no one remembers? Well, that would be the hard-luck guy from the United States named Jansen. And as far as I was concerned, it might as well have been forty-fourth.

Whatever the explanation, my performance absolutely devastated me. As I mentioned earlier, I went into semi-seclusion, thereby dooming myself for the 1,000 three days later. In truth, no one expected me to win, not Nick Thometz, not Woody Jansen, not Pete Mueller, not Robin Jansen, not Dan Jansen. I simply did not have what Dr. Loehr calls the proper "emotional connection" to the 1,000 in general—that would come later—and I certainly hadn't made the proper preparation for this race in particular.

I drew number 88 for the race—as if I needed to be reminded of the '88 Olympics. Following the strategy (and I use the word loosely) that Pete and I had discussed, I took off hard in an attempt to simply overpower the race. I skated the first 200 in 16.96, fastest in the field by far. At 600 meters I seemed to be in good shape at 44.63. I say "seemed" because I myself knew I was dead. I wasn't prepared either mentally or physically to win that race. I remember telling myself as I took the line, "Well, you never know," but I knew. Deep down, I knew. I tired badly and finished in twenty-sixth place, behind three of my teammates, Nick (fifteenth), Eric Flaim (sixteenth), and Dave Besteman (twentieth).

It was difficult to analyze the race. Uwe didn't skate because of the flu. Igor Zhelezovsky (by then with the Unified Team), probably the greatest 1,000-meter skater of all time, was sixth. Olaf Zinke of Germany, who had never won an international race before, took the gold, which to this day still confuses me. On the day that I had set the world record in the 500 in Davos, January 25, I was paired with Olaf in the 1,000, and starting on the outer, I actually beat him to the crossover, a rare occurrence. A South Korean named Kim Yoon-man, whom I had never even heard of, won the silver. Yukinori Miyabe of Japan, less of a surprise, took the bronze. The ice was much better than it had been for the 500, a fair race for all, I felt. Go figure.

A few days after the race, Gabes and I grabbed a few beers and drove up into the mountains, just the two of us. He hadn't performed up to expectations in his short-track events, either, and, like me, was feeling a little sorry for himself. But as we talked and talked, about our lives and our training, about Jane, about our victories and our defeats, we started feeling a little better. We realized that we were among the chosen, the people who were able to have dreams and realize those dreams in competition.

"Someday," said Gabes, "this will help us."

I hoped he was right.

—

I knew what my critics were saying after Albertville: Dan Jansen was a choker. The two falls in Calgary could be explained by the death of his sister, but there was no explanation for Albertville, when he seemed to be an absolute lock for a medal. Knowing that people felt that way about me hurt. It hurt a lot. But one thing I was not going to do was give up. Fortunately, we already knew that the next Winter Olympics, in Lillehammer, was only two years away instead of four, and that was a big mental boost. I continued to work with Dr. Loehr and my personal life continued to improve, especially when the best gift in the world came along, a little girl.

One of the first things Robin and I had talked about, of course, was having kids. I mean, I wouldn't have wanted my mother and father to get lonely—they only had twenty-four grandchildren. Robin's first thought was that she wanted to have five kids, while my idea was three. At this writing all I know is that we are ecstatically happy with the one we have.

We found out Robin was pregnant in September 1992. Coincidentally (or, some would say, predictably), Renee, her twin, conceived at almost the exact same time and eventually gave birth to a baby girl, Logan, just forty hours before Robin delivered Jane. (I told you they were close.) Like all couples, we started kicking around names during Robin's pregnancy, and one day "Jane" popped into my head. I mentioned it to Robin, and she got excited about it, too. We had other names in mind—if it was a boy, Jacob Daniel, J.D. to balance with D.J., was a strong possibility—but if it was a girl I knew that deep inside I wanted to honor the memory of my sister. But then my sensitivity kicked in. Would people think I was trying to attract attention to myself with that name? Would they think I was trying to cling to the past, and to the bad memories, in an unhealthy way? But finally we decided: Why should we care what anybody thought? It's an honor for Jane, and only that, and that's what we're going to do.

Our daughter was born on May 27, 1993, one of the most beautiful days of my life. I witnessed her birth in the delivery room. When we told my family her name was Jane, they all cried. I look forward to the day when I will sit down with Jane and tell her about the first Jane, and what a wonderful person her namesake was.

CHAPTER 6

Lillehammer:
The Day Before

I awakened feeling strong and positive on the seventeenth, a Thursday, the day before the 1,000. I had been talking to Dr. Loehr every day, and he had encouraged me to visualize all the good 1,000s I had skated during the year. And there were a lot of them. We figured that the best approach was to take it visually rather than strategically, because I seemed to have my best 1,000s that way, including the hand-timed 1:12.4 I had skated on the Hamar track in the pre-Olympic tune-up. In other words, I didn't concentrate on precisely *how* I was going to skate it, but, rather, more on how I would *feel* during the race. This may have disappointed some of the skating experts who faxed me analyses of what had gone wrong in the 500 and suggestions for what I should do in the 1,000. For example, one man told me to strap wooden stabilizers to the sides of my skates. And they say expert advice is hard to come by!

By this time, I'd be lying if I said I felt totally positive about winning the gold in the 1,000. In retrospect, I know that first place would've been the only thing to satisfy me in the 500. Had I gotten silver or bronze, it would've proven essentially the same thing as my eighth-place finish: Though Jansen was the best in the world, he was simply unable to show it in the Olympics. But, honestly, any kind of medal in the 1,000 would've made me feel complete. Maybe that put a little less pressure on me and made me feel more relaxed.

After a good training session, I spent most of the day at the house my family had rented. I did the usual things—played cribbage, laughed with Jane and Robin, munched pizza, and pretended I was completely cool, calm, and collected. At about 7 P.M., when it was time for me to return to the Village, I gathered the family together and spoke from the heart.

"Listen, guys, tomorrow is my last shot, my last Olympic race. And I want you to promise me that you're going to go out there and have fun because that's exactly what I plan to do. All the pressure, all the burdens of the past, forget about them. Skating has been my life for the last decade, and ninety-eight percent of my memories are positive. That's what I want this to be."

I meant every word of that speech. It was not a hedge in case I didn't get a medal. It was how I honestly felt. Skating had been both my master and my friend since I was a kid. It had taken me to all kinds of wonderful places, places I would never have seen if I had just been the tailback or the shortstop at West Allis Central High. My best friends in the world I had met through skating, and I had been on a skating-connected trip the night I met Robin. I wanted this last one to be a celebration of all those things, regardless of the outcome.

I went back to the USOC house, watched a little TV, then went to my room and read a few chapters of *The Client,* John Grisham's latest book. I would've been hanging out with Gabes, but the short-trackers were training in Oslo, so I stayed mostly to myself. A few people wished me luck, but there wasn't much to say. Before I went to bed I got a massage, then went to check my mail slot. Since I tried not to read the papers or watch much American TV, one of the ways I knew that my story was generating a lot of interest was that I had my own slot, as did Bonnie and Nancy Kerrigan and, I assume, Tonya Harding. Anyway, to my surprise, among the assorted messages in there was a fax from Jimmy Buffett that read simply: DAN, BLOW THE VOL-CANO!

Now, of all the things that could fire up a guy the night before his Olympic race, getting faxed by Jimmy Buffett, whom I had seen in concert several times and whom I had listened to a thousand times just lying in my boat on the lake, is at the top of my list. The reference he made was to one of his songs called, as it happens, "Volcano," and it was clear what he meant: "Blow the volcano" meant "Go for it all the way." Jimmy, I intended to.

My first thought was that Buffett had heard I was a fan and just faxed me out of the clear blue sky, but it hadn't happened that way. It turned out that Woody had called down to a bar in Key West owned by Buffett and asked if they could get a message to him.

"I don't know, man," the guy said. "He's not here."

"Well, if you could, just ask him to send some kind of inspirational note up to Dan Jansen," Mike said. And then he left the fax number for me in Lillehammer.

Now, what are the chances of Jimmy Buffett actually getting a message like that? You have to think that Buffett, who's not exactly a nine-to-five kind of guy, gets a lot of weird messages from a lot of weird people. And from what I know of his tropical lifestyle, speed skating is not exactly at the top of his list of concerns. Yet he got the message and came through, and I liked to think of it as a small miracle. I called over to the house and told them about it, and Jim said, "Man, you sound fired up. You sound ready." I was.

Before I went to sleep that night, I pulled out a note that Pete had given me after practice that day. Even though Pete is a person who will speak his mind, sometimes sentiments are best expressed in writing. And his note really moved me. "No matter what happens tomorrow," it read, "you will be remembered as one of the greats in this sport. Nothing can change that. You have my respect and my love."

A fax from Buffett. A note from the heart of Pete. The love of my family. I went to bed a happy, contented man. I had a real serene and peaceful feeling, unlike any feeling I'd ever had before an Olympic race. "I can win this race," I thought to myself. "I really can." I slept like a baby. Dr. Loehr would've liked to hear that.

● FEBRUARY 18, 1994

On the morning of the race a couple of interesting things happened that I didn't know about until later.

Pete got up real early and paid a visit to this small church in the village. The temperature was about thirty below, but he put on his parka and sucked it up. He's not a regular churchgoer, but he does pray and he does believe. Pete's prayer went something like this: "If You let Dan win the race, I will donate all my bonus money to the church." Pete's contract paid him extra money if his skaters medaled.

Over at my family's rented house, meanwhile, my brother Jim woke up with the strangest feeling. During the night, he said, he had felt like our sister Jane was in the room with him, not exactly like a visitation or a vision, but more like a presence. And Jane assured him, somehow, that I would win the race. As I've indicated before, Jim is the straightest shooter of the Jansens, the one least likely to follow superstition and things like that. But he felt this strongly. It was with some reluctance that he told our family members about it, and he really couldn't explain it any further when my sisters, who are more inclined to believe in such things, pressed him on it. He never told me about it until weeks after the race, but it affected him deeply and he still thinks about it today. I've had dreams when all of a sudden Jane would just appear, but I've never felt anything like Jim described.

Both Pete and Jim would've been feeling considerably less confident had they been able to read my thoughts when I went out to warm up about ninety minutes before the race, however. I just felt "off." That's the only way to describe it: "off." There was nothing wrong with me physically, and, as far as I could tell, I was 100 percent mentally, too. But the timing wasn't there. Sometimes when you skate everything just flows real easily. But other times it seems forced and labored, almost as if rust had somehow collected in the well-oiled machine. My skates felt almost round, like hockey skates, which are designed for quick turns, as opposed to the flatter shape of the speed skate. When I put them down they just weren't secure on the ice. I'm not sure I can equate what I was feeling to any other sport. Maybe it's like the football placekicker who feels strong and ready but nevertheless seems to be missing his steps and pulling everything to the right.

This would've been as good a time as any to panic, but for some reason I didn't. I guess it was because, nerves-wise, I felt fine. It wasn't an entire body break-down but seemed to be centered in the legs. Then it dawned on me that perhaps I needed to feel more tired. That wouldn't seem to make any sense, except that in World Cup meets we skate a 500 before a 1,000. And though you might feel a little fatigued after that, you also feel completely loose. So I decided, an hour before my last Olympic race, to get myself a little tired. The danger, as Dr. Loehr said later, was disturbing a routine that up to that point had worked extremely well. But to pretend that nothing was wrong would've been a fatal error.

I didn't exactly come clean to Pete. "I don't feel real normal out there, I don't feel great," I told him.

"Nah," he said. "It looks good, it looks real good."

He meant it, too. It did look good. It just didn't *feel* good.

So instead of sitting around and thinking back in the dressing room, my normal prerace routine, I hopped onto the stationary bike. There were a few guys back there spinning, but I really went after it, using a lot of energy, really working up a sweat, as if it were an off-day drill. I remember only one conversation back there. A Norwegian skater, Adne Søndrål, came by, shook my hand, and said, "Good luck, I hope you win." Since he was in the 1,000, too, I really thought that was a nice thing to say.

I was on the bike for maybe fifteen intense minutes or so, and then I went out for a jog. It was freezing outside, but I was sweating and it felt good. So when I came back, I felt better but still not completely in sync.

In retrospect, I think I would've been more panicked if I had felt like this before the 500. The expectations were so much greater in that race, and there is a much smaller margin of error. Then, too, the 1,000 field was wide open. Eric Heiden, who was commenting for CBS, said that at least ten skaters were capable of winning the gold in the 1,000. I think his estimate was a little high, but I could name at least six, Jansen being among them. Eric also said, "Dan's got to get out of his mind that this is the Olympics." Thanks, Eric. Exactly how was I supposed to do that?

My own feeling was that the skaters to beat were my old buddy and rival Igor Zhelezovsky and the Russian Sergei Klevchenya, who were going off in the first pair. I took my spot behind the starter to watch them. "Whatever happens," I thought, "it will be over soon."

And another thought flashed through my mind: "I really *do* love the 1,000." Seemed to me I had heard that someplace before.

CHAPTER 7

Lillehammer:
The Race

●FEBRUARY 18, 1994

My hunch about Igor and Sergei was correct. Igor turned in a 1:12.72 and Sergei a 1:12.85, with a small slip. Actually, I was a little surprised by the result because I thought Sergei had the advantage. He started on the first inner, which means he would also finish on the inner and could draft off Igor, who is a real fast closer. But it didn't happen that way, and if I've learned one thing in my career it's that anything can happen in the Olympics. Anyway, they posted the best times of the first six skaters, and, when it was my turn, in the fourth pair, I knew that Igor's was the time to beat.

Their times told me that the ice had to be good. Truthfully, I thought it was a little hard and I still didn't feel like I was gripping it very well. I kept those thoughts from Pete, though. To be honest, winning a gold medal at this point seemed, if not impossible, a long shot at best. And I think that was the consensus from everyone else, too. After all that had happened in Calgary and Albertville and in the 500 here, most of my family members had pretty much scaled down their hopes from "I hope he wins the gold" to "I just hope he skates a good race." Later, J.B. was honest enough to admit that he hadn't thought I was going to win, and Nick had had his doubts, too. As for my brother Jim, who had awakened with the most positive feelings of anyone, he had felt so sick with nervousness earlier in the day that he'd had to spend a couple hours in bed. Sometimes I think athletics are harder on the spectators than the competitors. But only sometimes.

As I approached the line I touched my hand to the ring I wore around my neck, a ritual I had begun during the season. It contained baby Jane's birthstone, an emerald. I took my position, starting on the outside lane with Junichi Inoue on the inside. I was calm, but my mind was racing. I don't think I've ever had a race where so many thoughts were going in and out of my mind. I thought briefly about my sister Jane, and that led me to think about baby Jane. She had slept through the 500 but was awake, I learned later, for the entire 1,000. Maybe she knew something none of the rest of us knew. And then I thought of my family and how much they were pulling for me and how nervous they must've been. If I thought at all about this probably being my last competitive race, I don't remember it.

I knew that the vast majority of spectators, people watching on television and even quite a few of my competitors, were pulling for me. That was an odd feeling, one that very few athletes in individual sports have ever felt. It made me feel good, of course, but it also added an obvious element of tension, particularly since, right up until I took my mark, I still felt my timing was off.

But suddenly, right before I heard the gun, a jolt of energy came into my legs. All those feelings of physical insecurity just fell away. I don't know why. Maybe my prerace strategy of bicycling and jogging had helped, maybe I just willed myself into it, or maybe someone was looking out for me. But I knew I was ready.

"Go!"

And I went. There was no reason to hold back, no need to skate a conservative race. The time I had to beat was out there, and it was a good one. I was no longer scared of the last lap in the 1,000 because the strength and the will were there. *I love the 1,000.*

Later, Pete said that he had not been pleased with the first half of my first corner. He'd thought I was slipping and that I'd shortened my stride ever so slightly. If I had, I'd done so subconsciously. My split at 200 meters was 16.71—anything under 17 is flying.

I settled into a real good rhythm right away on the straightaways, so my only thought became *Don't overpush the turns. You're still not gripping real well, so get solid in the turns, and make up the time in the straightaways.* I felt powerful and smooth, and fatigue wasn't a factor. *I love the 1,000.* I just seemed to be sailing through the race, in complete control.

But, suddenly, on the second-to-last inner turn, about 300 meters from the finish, I slipped briefly and my left hand shot toward the ice. It was the same turn on which Sergei had almost gone down in the first pair. I didn't realize this until later, but there was an audible collective gasp from the audience. My father thought to himself, "Oh, no, not again." Variations on that thought, I'm sure, were racing through the rest of my family's minds, too.

But for some reason I stayed very calm. I remember thinking, even though I must've done it in the flash of an eye: *Don't panic and start trying to get out of this thing all at once. Stay within yourself.* I had won about ten World Cup 1,000s over the years, the majority within the past six months, and it wasn't all that rare to win one with a slip. It's funny, but a couple of weeks before the Games, Pete had told the press, "Believe it or not, the thousand is an easier race for Dan. At five hundred meters, you can't make a mistake. At a thousand meters you can make a small mistake and still win." So the key was to keep the mistake "small."

Later, when I saw the slip in reverse slow motion, however, I simply could not believe it. Not only was the slip much more dramatic than I had thought, but I had come within an inch of stepping on one of the lane markers. You step on a block, you're down. Period. Had I done that, the triple crown of misfortune would've been mine for all time.

Why did I slip? Hard to say. Maybe it was inevitable because of my gripping problems. Maybe I was a little fatigued at the pace I was on, which, after all, was un-precedented. Maybe it was Fate stepping in one final time and saying, "Not so fast, D.J. You've got one more big test." But let me emphasize here that slips are not falls. I'm sure that many people think that that dreaded four-letter word F-A-L-L is always in a skater's mind, but it's just not so. Though some people associate me only with my falls in Calgary, I bet I hadn't gone down twice since then. Yes, falls are disasters. But slips are more commonplace, and you have to deal with them.

Because of a new rule mandating that coaches have to stand in the backstretch, I actually got my 600-meter time after the slip. In other races, I'd frequently had Bonnie standing by to give me the lap time a lot earlier, but that wasn't allowed in the Olympics. So as I raced by after the slip, Pete held up a card that said 26.5, which was the time for my first 400-meter lap. Nor-mally, even in a real good race, I'll have maybe a 27.1 or 27.2. Making a quick calculation with my 200-meter time, I knew I was in excellent shape, even with the slip. My actual time at 600 meters was 43.28, a world-record pace. I didn't hear the announcement, but I did hear the roar of the crowd.

Once I recovered, I had only one thought in my

mind: *Stay low over the last 200 meters and keep that left arm solid behind the back so it's not flopping.* If Pete and I talked about one thing before the race, it was that. Then, coming out of the last turn with fifty meters to go, I dropped both arms and just went for it, blew that volcano. I was extremely relaxed, in perfect rhythm, yet I was going for pure speed.

The crowd noise was deafening as I crossed the finish line, so I knew the time was good. Normally, I can tell by my legs whether or not it's been a good race. Sometimes I feel completely spent and my legs just burn, which probably means that I was a little too fatigued to have a great race. This time I felt almost nothing, just maybe a very small fatigue in my legs.

My first thought when I crossed the line was: That's a medal. I don't know what type, but that's a medal. For a couple of seconds I struggled to pull off the hood of my uniform. I wear contacts, and sometimes it takes me a while to find and then focus on the clock. I looked and looked, but the crowd saw it before I did. Finally, there it was.

1:12.43! 1:12.43!

The time was fifty-eight hundredths of a second better than I had ever skated in the 1,000. And best of all were those two magic letters right next to it: WR. World Record. I raised my arms, closed my eyes, and covered them with my hands.

I guess the first thing I felt was disbelief. Had this happened in the 500, it would've been perfectly logical. But not in the 1,000, not with the way I'd felt before the race. There were several other pairs after me, but, truthfully, I knew I had it. I wish I could adequately describe my feelings when I saw Pete skating toward me, wearing what he called his lucky jean jacket (he had forgotten it for the 500 and felt guilty about it), his arms out. But I can't. We circled the oval with his arm around my waist. "You did it," he kept saying. "You showed 'em all. You showed 'em you can win the big one." That was not the first thought in my mind, but, yes, I guess I did. What Pete momentarily forgot was that my victory had just earned a tidy sum of money for the Christ Church in Mequon, Wisconsin, where he lives. Those had been the terms of his early morning prayer, and later he felt glad to meet them. Pete later told me that my medal meant more to him than the one he had earned for himself in 1976. "I was too young to appreciate it then, D.J.," he said. "It didn't come easily for me, but it did come pretty quickly. Only a few of us know what it took to get this one." He spoke with absolute sincerity, and I have no reason to believe he wasn't telling the truth.

I didn't learn about all the reactions until later. Robin shouted, "Thank you, God." She then began hyperventilating and had to get attention at the medical stand. My father's reaction wasn't quite that extreme, but he did stand up and raise his arms to the sky. Boy, was Mom blocked out that day. I know what my family was feeling—relief for me, relief that I wouldn't have to spend the next few months apologizing for letting everyone down. Dr. Loehr had trained his binoculars on me the whole race, and, when it was over, it took him a while to realize that tears were streaming down his face.

Back home, my brother Dick was trying like heck to avoid the results, but Eric, his son, kept watching TV and giving him commentary. "Don't tell me, Eric," Dick said. "I don't want to know." But when they announced the world record, Eric let out a shout and Dick knew it was good news. Then he ran to the TV. Robin made her phone calls first, and it was her sister who informed Woody. I wish he could've been over there with me, but that didn't diminish his joy. "I felt like I was walking on air the whole day," he told me later.

My sisters who were home in West Allis, Diane and Joanne, had identical experiences that day. Wherever my sisters went, people felt compelled to tell them exactly where they were and what they had been doing when they heard the news about the world record. "Six years earlier, we heard where everyone was when Dan fell," said Diane. "And now we heard where everyone was when he won." It was a little more information than they really needed. Rick Smith, my lawyer buddy, was en route to his office in Milwaukee when the news came over the radio. Suddenly, all around him, people raised their arms and honked their horns, a rare moment of communion in a traffic jam.

Some of the reports that made me smile the widest happened right in Lillehammer. When the news was announced over at the hockey arena, the Austrians and Finns sounded cowbells in celebration. Brian Boitano, the American figure skater, who's a really great guy, raised his hand in a salute. And in a hotel room in Oslo, where he was watching the 1,000 alone, Andy Gabel shook his fist at the TV and said, "You got one, D.J. You got one." Suddenly, dozens and dozens of skaters, not just his American teammates but skaters from other countries, showed up at his room to offer their congratulations. "I felt like *I* won the gold, D.J.," he told me later.

Robin, once she recovered, was over in the stands holding Janie and pointing at me. "Look, there's Daddy! There's Daddy!" From that distance, Jane didn't know Daddy from Haakon and Kristin, the official Olympic mascots she got to meet later. Finally, I was able to skate over to Robin, and it was an incredibly emotional experience. "It's over, D.J.," she kept yelling. "It's over. Now you've got both of them." She meant world records in both the 500 and 1,000. I said nothing. I was too busy crying. Pete later told me that I was a bigger wreck after winning the 1,000 than I was after losing the 500. I'm sure that's true. I knew what losing in the Olympics felt like. But winning? I never knew it would feel this good.

Finally, I made it back to the locker room, with a doctor from the USOC following me around to make sure nobody slipped me anything—I still had to go through drug testing. It was at that point that I started drinking cups of water because my history is to have trouble, uh, performing for the urine test. Then it was time for the medals ceremony. As it happened, on the night before the 500-meter race, Elin Kristoffersen, the Norwegian woman from whom my family rented their house, who was a volunteer worker at the Olympics, had ironed the American flag, so sure was she that it would be the one going up after the race. I don't think she did any ironing before the 1,000, but, unpressed or not, boy, did that flag look good! I knew that hearing the national anthem would be emotional, and although I cried and stumbled through the words, I actually controlled myself better than I thought I would. I glanced at my medal a few times to make sure it was still there. I don't know how many different things raced through my mind, but halfway through the anthem I started thinking about my sister Jane and hoping she was watching. On the last two notes of the anthem, I looked up at the sky and saluted. That was for you, Jane, then and forever.

After the ceremony, an official came up to me and said, "You know, there's a victory lap with the Olympic mascots." Not having taken one before, I didn't realize it. In fact, my skates were down in the locker room and somebody had to run down to get them real quick. The funny thing is, months before the Olympics Robin and I had discussed how nice it would be if I could take kind of an unofficial victory lap with Janie in my arms. (We both thought, however, it would be after the 500-meter race.) It was just sort of dreaming, and we'd never discussed it beyond that. But there I was. The lights in the arena were off and they were playing "The Skater's Waltz" and people were singing softly and flashbulbs were popping and it was so quiet, almost like church, that you could hear our blades scraping on the ice. And suddenly I looked up, and there was Janie hanging out over the ice. Robin, relentless as ever, had passed her down ten rows of spectators until a security guard finally handed her to me. Why Jane wasn't terrified by this scene, I don't know, but she was smiling and looking around as if this were the most normal activity in the world.

For the first few steps of that lap, I concentrated on staying up more than I ever had in any competitive race. I had my daughter in one arm, flowers in the other, two small kids in costume skating beside me, and timing devices sitting out on the ice that I had to avoid. *Don't fall, D.J. Whatever you do, don't fall.* But then I started to relax. I glanced at Janie and she looked like an angel, a little smile on her face, her eyes wide with excitement and maybe a little confusion, a stickum American flag on her cheek that Robin had pasted there that morning. A journalist later told me that up in the press box some of the most cynical guys he knows had tears in their eyes. I often wonder if, somehow, some way, that moment will register as Jane's first memory, that some part of her will recall the beautiful darkness and the sound of skates against ice and everybody singing. That would be nice.

I know it will never leave me. The circumstances that had brought me to that moment, with the whole world watching, had essentially begun with Jane's death on February 14, 1988. And here we were, six years later, another Jane in my arms, tasting victory at last. I had, indeed, come full circle.

At the press conference following the victory lap, I got a call from President Clinton. The first thing that happened was that I got put on hold. Somehow, that made me feel better. If an athlete gets a call from a busy president, he should get put on hold. As the reporters gathered around, I took it on the mobile phone. Here's what I said:

"Hello, yes sir. I'm just wonderful, thank you, thanks a lot. . . . It's been a long time coming. . . . Yes, I understand. . . . I haven't seen it yet. . . . I met your wife and daughter the other day. . . . Sorry I didn't win it then. . . . They can watch it on TV. . . . Thanks very much. . . . I appreciate it." I told the reporters that he said the whole country was pulling for me and that I was struck by how genuinely happy he seemed for me. Later, I talked to the First Lady, who called me from a plane heading, fittingly, to Wisconsin. I know she felt good because she had seen firsthand how bad I'd felt after the 500.

I talked for almost an hour at the press conference until a USOC doctor suddenly grabbed me and said, "Come on! We've got less than two minutes to get to doping or you'll be disqualified." By that time I had to go to the bathroom so badly I was ready to explode, so I bolted out of that room like a racehorse out of the gate at Churchill Downs. Never has a urine sample been given with so much enthusiasm.

Norwegian television wanted to fly me back to the main staging area in Lillehammer for more press conferences, but I told them, "Not unless you want to fly my whole family. It's time for them." And it was. I wanted to be with the people who had shared so much pain and agony with me over the last decade. The family had planned a celebration after the 500, and when it hadn't happened, they'd decided not to tempt fate and organize another one before the 1,000. So when we got back to the house we had to order out for beer, champagne, and pizza. Spontaneous parties are always the best kind, anyway. Assorted press people found their way to the house, but that was okay, because I could talk to them and celebrate with my family at the same time. I don't think anyone had a better time than my brother Jim, who held the cue cards for the people from the David Letterman show. They wanted me to go on live and say the final entry from that night's Top Ten list. The category was: Top Ten Things Norwegians Call Americans. And my line was: Bobbitteers. In case I started to take myself too seriously, there was always Letterman.

It would be impossible to completely cover the range of emotions I was feeling. But as I look back, I'm sure the primary one was thankfulness. I was thankful all the pressure was over, thankful my family could stop living with this Olympic nightmare and stop feeling sorry for me, thankful I had a wonderful wife and child to experience this with me, thankful my sister Jane would not be forgotten.

You know, I remember reading once that Roger Bannister, the man who broke the four-minute-mile mark in 1954, said he had continued to compete in the mile mainly because he had failed to get a gold medal in the 1,500 meters in the 1952 Olympics in Helsinki (he had finished fourth). Had he won the gold, he said, he probably would have retired right away. But years later, this man, who had performed one of the most fabled achievements in all of sports, said that in retrospect, he would have rather had the gold medal than the first four-minute mile. That speaks volumes about how athletes feel about gold medals.

When I woke the next morning, tired but still ecstatic, Robin leaned over to me and said, "Guess what? It wasn't a dream."

CHAPTER 8

The Future

The Olympics officially ended for me when I was elected to carry the American flag in the closing ceremonies. The team captains in each sport made the selection, and I was chosen from a group that included Bonnie, short-tracker Cathy Turner, and skier Liz McIntyre. Being recognized by your peers is the biggest honor you can have, and I appreciated it deeply.

But my competitive career had one more stop—the season's final World Cup event in Heerenveen, Holland, three weeks after Lillehammer. Imagine if you're a member of the Chicago Bulls and a few weeks after you win the NBA championship you've got to go back and play a playoff game. That's how I felt. My preparation, as you might imagine, was less than thorough. I did get onto the ice for a few days in the second week following Lillehammer, but right before I went to Holland, I had appearances in three different cities in three nights. I left Wednesday night for Holland, arrived on Thursday, and competed on Saturday and Sunday. I surprised myself when I got a second in both 500s and a first in the 1,000. I didn't have to place nearly that high to win the overall World Cup championship, so my victory was decisive, an affirmation of how well the whole season had gone.

Actually, I would've felt bad if I hadn't competed. First of all, I'd made a commitment and I'm not in the habit of standing people up. But, second, the people in Holland are such skating fans, maybe the best in the world, that I felt like I owed it to them. When I was a young kid training and competing in Europe, it was in Holland that I first realized the strange dichotomy of being a U.S. speed skater—you're a no-name at home and a hero abroad.

But the weekend did have an anticlimactic feel to it. Even when I was at the starting line, I couldn't shake the feeling of *What am I doing here? I don't belong here anymore. Let's move on.* I skated on automatic pilot, which, as it turned out, wasn't that bad. But if it turns out that Heerenveen is my last race—and it probably was—it was a great place to go out.

So much has happened since Lillehammer that, as I complete this manuscript, in June 1994, I still haven't had time to reflect on my future. Obviously, the '94 Olympics and, by extension, those in Calgary and Albertville will always be a strong current through my life and the lives of my family members. When you're in a pressure-filled competition like the Olympics, you try to shut out the rest of the world, so I really had no idea of the full impact of my 1,000-meter race until I came home.

I went directly from Lillehammer to the ESPYs, the ESPN sports awards, in New York, and was simply amazed when famous athletes asked me for *my* autograph. That just doesn't happen to speed skaters. I remember the day I threw out the first pitch before a Milwaukee Brewers game a few years ago and I was fired up for a week because Paul Molitor came by and said,

"Hi, Dan." The surprises continued. I went on the Letterman show a few days later and got a standing ovation. The phone rang nonstop at the offices of ISI, my new representatives, with literally hundreds of groups asking me to make speeches.

Letters arrived by the bushel, and they're still coming. Some come from as far away as California with just "Dan Jansen" on the envelope. Robin said to the postman, "If I get a digit wrong at Christmas they send the package back, but my husband gets letters from two time zones removed without even a state." Many of the letters were exceptional, but we were really touched by one sent from a woman in Norway. It said: "Before the Olympics, we Norwegians had three wishes—good weather, many medals for Norway, and that Dan Jansen would take home a gold." They got all three. That is the essence of sportsmanship, a code of behavior that knows no national boundaries. One memento I received from an Indian reservation always makes me smile. It's a big banner that now hangs in the Pettit Center that says: "Creator Smiles on You. To Us You Are: 'zhoosh-kwaada'e wiiji-ombaashi. He skates with the wind.' "

I'm no Michael Jordan in the fame department, but

since Lillehammer I rarely go anywhere without being recognized as Dan Jansen. This is a little different than it used to be when a certain percentage of the people who recognized me would get this confused look on their face and start stammering, "Hey, you're . . . you're . . ." That was the price of being on TV once every four years. Of course, even after Lillehammer, there's still some trouble with my name. I don't know how many people have said to me, "David Jansen, what a pleasure to meet you." "Thank you," I say, "and if you'll excuse me, I have to continue my search for the one-armed man."

Oh, one other thing about my victory—I got asked to play Batman in an ice show. I declined. I'm holding out for Superman.

One of the best moments came when I was officially welcomed home with a parade that was televised live in the Milwaukee area. (Actually, it was my third homecoming parade.) It ended back at the Pettit Center and gave me the proper forum in which to publicly thank my parents for teaching me both how to win and how to lose. It still chokes up my mother that I did that, and I meant every word. A couple from the local skating club did a wonderful thing when they gave my parents their own gold medal that says: "To Gerry and Harry Jansen, gold medal parents." Truer words were never spoken.

So what now? That's the question I started to hear most frequently after a few months. The people closest to me don't bother to ask because they know my answer: I don't know. Most of them figure that my final competitive race was the meet in Holland and, as I write this, that is the strongest possibility. I actually heard someone say not long ago, "Jeez, Dan Jansen finally makes it to the top and he retires?" *Finally?* I've been at or near the top of my sport for a decade, so it's not like I just got there.

Even Robin was trying to trick me into tipping my hand about competing. We have a trust fund that is contingent upon my skating, and Robin said to me one day, "Should I close this thing out?" We have a Jeep that is mine only if I'm in competition, and Robin asked, "Should I renew the license on this?" I always tell her the same thing: "After I decide myself, honey, you'll be the first to know." Interestingly, Pete Mueller has a theory that I could continue to compete and even dominate both my events right through the 1998 Olympics.

Pete, we'll never get to test that theory because it just isn't going to happen. But thanks anyway.

The only thing standing in my way from officially retiring is the world sprint championships set for February 1995 in the Pettit Center. Naturally, there's a lot of pressure for me to compete, and part of me would love to oblige the American skating community as a way of saying thank you for years of support. On the other hand, just showing up and competing is not fair, either. If I'm there, I want to be at my best, and my training schedule has all but been destroyed by my post-Olympic commitments.

So, as you read this, either I'll have one more meet or I'll be finished. And that leaves a whole lot of years to do something else.

Coaching is a possibility, though for now it would only be at the junior level and in an unofficial capacity. Beyond that, I don't know. Pete is no longer the national team coach, having resigned right after the Olympics, but the job is in good hands because Nick Thometz, at this writing, will be taking over, possibly as the program director, definitely as sprint coach. Nick is organized, he has a program he believes in, and from the standpoint of the federation, he's easier to work with than Pete. He certainly got everything he could out of Bonnie during the year he spent with her.

One of the few regrets that both Nick and I have about leaving the competitive side of the sport is that Nick didn't get the opportunity to coach me. It would've been interesting since I think we have similar ideas about skating. And although Nick at one time was so quiet he made me look like a blabbermouth, his personality has become much more outgoing and forceful since he's been a coach. I don't know whether he could've pulled the same effort out of me that Pete did, but it's possible.

If I became a coach, I really don't think I'd need a personality change. Although I'm basically quiet, my history in sports is that competition brings me out a little bit. In football, for example, I was always a leader on the field, if not in the locker room, and that's the most important thing. My strength as a coach would lie, I think, in my ability to take apart a person's technique and see what little flaws needed to be fixed. Along those same lines, the hardest thing for me would be to keep in mind that not every skater can make a quick transfer from coach's instruction to on-the-ice technique. That was one of the gifts that I had, and I know Bonnie, to name just one, was the same way. That is the one reason that world-class competitors don't necessarily make world-class coaches; there would have to be some realization that things don't come easy for everybody. But I think, over time, I would make that adjustment.

Anyway, that's all talk and theory because at this time I have no coaching plans on the national team level. There's so much travel involved that if I were coaching I might as well be competing.

One of the things I do hope to do is continue to be a presence in speed skating. I've been criticized over the years—with some validity, I suppose—for not speaking out on issues. It's funny, but some of the people closest to me are outspoken. Lord knows Pete has let his opinions be known over the years, and Bonnie, Andy, and Nick are all on the speed-skating association's governing board. Neither Bonnie nor I was even captain of the Olympic speed-skating team, and some people found that strange. It wasn't. For me the job was just not a priority. The main duty of the Olympic team captains is to select a flag bearer for the opening ceremonies; I knew I wouldn't be attending them anyway because my race was only two days later. That is not to take away from Brian Wanek, who was a terrific captain for us.

As for not being outspoken during my career, well, all I can say is that I honestly felt fortunate just being in the position I was in. Aside from the time when Bonnie, Nick, and I lobbied to get Pete back, I couldn't bring myself to complain or find fault with the association. As far as I was concerned, I was there to skate and I felt like the luckiest guy in the world just to have that opportunity. I suppose it has a lot to do with the way I was brought up. My mom and dad just always seemed thankful for what they had, and though they never talked about it, they did a good job of transferring that feeling to me.

That doesn't mean I think everything is perfect with our association. Andy feels that too many people in the decision-making process base their judgments on what's good for their own kid rather than what's good for the sport as a whole. But this is a problem that isn't likely to go away. The board consists of volunteers who give their time without compensation or recognition, and it takes a special person to think altruistically.

I don't think we should build the sport into something it's not. Speed skating has never been and never will be a sport that's going to generate an enormous amount of revenue. But it is incumbent upon the association to do a better job of luring corporate sponsorship. That was one of the things Pete was always harping on. Our downhill skiers, for example, have a lot of dollars behind them, maybe because skiing is considered a sexy sport and a lot of corporate types do it. But over the past thirty years American speed skaters have won more medals than athletes in the other winter sports combined.

I hope our success continues, but these are not the brightest times for speed skating's future. When Eric Heiden retired, there was a bunch of people like Nick, Eric Flaim, and me waiting in the wings. That's not the case now. And it's probably worse in the women's division, since Bonnie will probably retire after the Worlds in February 1995. She has stood absolutely alone among the American women for the last six years. I know one thing: The rest of the world is going to keep improving. Eric Heiden's individual accomplishments will never be surpassed, yet the vast majority of skaters in the field now beat the 38.03 he put up to win the 500-meter gold in Lake Placid.

One thing the association must get tougher on is mandating that Olympic candidates train with the Olympic coach. When I was coming up, my personal coach was always the national team coach, and that's the way it should be. Skaters who listen to one voice for three years can't suddenly get accustomed to a different voice just for the Olympics.

I'm certainly not advocating an overhaul of the system. A fine-tuning, maybe, but not an overhaul. The Eastern Bloc way of doing things, i.e., find a kid at an early age, push him into a sport, feed him a regimented, this-way-or-the-highway program, was proven not to have been the answer and led to a whole series of problems, not the least of which was steroids. I was always proud to be an American, to have the freedom to live the way I wanted, and to have a life beyond what went on at the 400-meter oval. But the fact remains that speed skaters should have more secure financial backing, and now, with the success Bonnie and I had in Lillehammer, seems like the perfect time to go after it.

Even talking about the subject of money makes me uncomfortable, though I know that increasingly it seems to be the number one subject of professional sports. When I read the sports pages these days I think

I'm reading *The Wall Street Journal,* and it was always a source of pride for me that I competed in a sport that, by and large, was purely amateur.

That's why the commercially oriented analyses that took place right after the Olympics were by far the worst thing—maybe the only bad thing—that happened as a result of my winning the gold medal. As soon as I got back to the States all I read was how much Bonnie and alpine skier Tommy Moe and Nancy Kerrigan and Dan Jansen were going to make from the Olympics. You can take this with however many grains of salt you want, but I never thought for one moment what winning the gold medal would mean to my bank account.

Some of the stories made me laugh. One analyst wrote, "Jansen is going to hit the marketplace with thunder and lightning. What's noteworthy is Dan is sort of a virgin in the marketplace." It's always nice to be described as "sort of" a virgin as opposed to, say, a full-fledged virgin. But the comment that will always stick with me is one made by a reporter who, at the end of an otherwise positive article, talked about the "financial killing" I would make off my gold medal, and added: "Not bad for a guy who's one for seven."

Remember how I told you that comment about tripping made by the woman in the bar didn't bother me because it was so ignorant? Well, this is the flip side of that. It was made by a journalist, someone who should know better, and it does make me angry because it reduces an entire career—in this case mine—to the eight races this guy happened to know about. There was no thought given to my seven World Cup overalls, to my two world sprint championships, to my eight world records. Further, it hints that in some way, shape, or form, I would be getting monies from the Olympics on false pretenses, that I hadn't *earned* the right to be compensated for the gold medal, despite the fact that I've dedicated virtually my whole life to my sport. I think the public is so saturated with the concept of athlete-as-millionaire these days that some perspective is needed, particularly in the so-called Olympic sports like my own.

Speed skaters tend to come from mostly middle-class backgrounds. Obviously, there are not many deprived kids from urban areas, as there are in, say, basketball and boxing. It's a sport that requires parental participation and, at the very least, gas money. But neither is speed skating a sport like tennis or golf, which rich kids from country-club families tend to dominate. There are a few families that are wealthy, but the overwhelming majority are very much working-class. For example, Gabes's father is a surgeon, but Bonnie, Nick, and J.B. are, like me, working-class kids.

Certainly there is no way I could've done it without my parents making major sacrifices in their life. Had I been forced to take a full-time job, my training and competition schedules would've been destroyed, and I would've gone from world champion to also-ran very quickly. And had I lived on my own, paying for my own apartment and meals without a full-time job, it would've been a real struggle to get by. In the early years of my career, I probably made about $12,000 per year, mostly prize money, which finally, over the last decade, our Olympic Committee came to realize was necessary. True, I had no dependents, but as anybody in the real world knows, $12,000 is not a lot of money. I'm not complaining about it, but remember that I was among the elite in the entire world in my sport. A lot of people were making considerably *less* than $12,000. Translate that to a more mainstream sport, or even the business world, and you'll see that it's not much money.

Endorsements? I did an M & M's commercial before the '84 Olympics that was part of a series using U.S.

Olympians. It was fun and I appreciated it and it has certainly provided a few moments of family humor when everyone sees how young I look, but it was hardly a financial windfall. And that about covers the national endorsement department. I had a few modest local deals and made a little bit of money making speeches. The other day I was wearing a Reebok shirt, and somebody said to me, "Wow, you must be getting a bundle to wear that." And I said, "Well, maybe Shaquille O'Neal's getting a bundle, but what I'm getting is a free T-shirt." And this is after I had competed in *four* Olympics. Heck, until about 1988, I paid for my own skates.

Part of the reason I didn't get more was my own reticence. A lot of people told me I could've made a killing after the '88 Olympics, but I always felt a little guilty about it because of the circumstances. Even when I would get paid for an appearance, which is a legitimate enterprise, I wondered if people were thinking, "Oh, he's making money off his sister's death." If that's oversensitivity, well, so be it. That's how I felt. Anyway, until fairly recently I was deathly afraid of public speaking, so it wasn't like I was savoring a career as an orator anyway.

It was around 1988 when my income started to go

up. The Miller Brewing Company was one of several corporations that started a jobs program to support Olympic athletes. That paid me about $20,000. And when I got involved with Bennett Raffer, my first manager, his group paid me about another $20,000. Again, with prize money and appearances, my income was probably about $50,000 per year from 1988 through 1992. Then, in the last two years, the USOC came up with an excellent program called "Team 94," which was put together after Albertville. It was designed to keep the top athletes around since there were only two years until Lillehammer. It was a performance-based incentive program that paid what was for speed skaters serious prize money. A first place in a World Cup race, for example, was $5,000. With four races, a skater had the potential to make $20,000 in one weekend. The same thing was going on in other sports. So in the last two years my income has been close to $100,000 a year.

Talking about my personal finances makes me extremely uncomfortable, and the only reason I'm discussing it is to provide some perspective. I'm certainly not complaining about making $50,000 a year, which gives you a more-than-comfortable lifestyle in and around Milwaukee, Wisconsin. There are people raising families on considerably less than that. But on the other hand, I was among the best in the world in my sport, and I'm certainly not going to feel guilty about it. I guarantee you that athletes in our sport work ten times as hard as 90 percent of the professional athletes who are making millions.

Anyway, my larger point is this: I was one of the lucky ones. I had the job from Miller, some earning power through endorsements and appearances, the ability to win the World Cup prize money, and an understanding and loving family. Dozens of others in our sport barely scrape by.

So, when I hear that the Olympics was only about money—*Not bad for someone who's one for seven*—it really makes my blood boil. Yes, my income has gone up considerably since Lillehammer. But I guarantee that what I put into this sport—the blood, sweat, and tears that have flowed over the last decade—came down to more than one race, as magical as that race might've been.

I'm now convinced more than ever that the victory is in the struggle. That might be hard for the guy who wrote the "one for seven" line to understand, but it's true. Think about it: The percentage of athletes who compete and don't win a medal, never mind getting a second's worth of recognition, is unbelievably high. The teamwork, the setting of goals, the competition are what count. How many hundreds of athletes remain in their sport for years despite the fact that gold medals, endorsement contracts, even simple recognition by the public are not only elusive goals but probably nonexistent ones? If I have one thing to be thankful for, it's that I had the opportunity to succeed. Yes, I came dangerously close to being known as perhaps the most prominent nonmedalist of all time. But I also had the opportunity to be one of the most successful Olympians of all time.

What else did my victory mean? Well, Pete Mueller is absolutely convinced that it had a higher purpose, maybe one that defies understanding. After watching the tape he swears that something, a power greater than myself, kept me up when I was about to fall in the 1,000-meter race. He told me later: "Dan, I believe everybody's here for a reason. There's a plan for everyone, and yours is going to be to impress upon the world that you don't give up, that after defeat you trudge on, and when you're defeated again, you keep going, and when you're defeated again you keep on going until you finally succeed. There's a larger picture at work, and you're part of it."

Well, that's a lot to swallow. I told Dr. Loehr about Pete's theory, and he admits that he is of two minds about it. On the one hand, his scientific background resists an interpretation predicated on outside forces. Everything in Dr. Loehr's training says that my ultimate success was based on careful physical training, a balanced, carefully monitored program of training and recovery, and, most important, a mental adjustment that enabled me to accept the premise that I could be the best in the 1,000. But he also told me, "There's a part of me that feels I'm involved in something extraordinary, that forces beyond our reach were at work." Like Pete, Dr. Loehr sees something like a test in all I went through. Why would Jane have to die on the very morning of the race in Calgary? Why would the ice have to turn soft in Albertville? Why would it have to break away at the precise moment it did in the 500 in Lillehammer?

It's very hard to react to those sentiments. Sometimes it's difficult for me to believe that it all could've been a coincidence. It does seem like a plan, that there was a purpose to it. But as soon as you say something like that, you commit the ultimate act of arrogance, which is to say that God tapped you on the shoulder and said, "Show us something." I feel very, very uncomfortable with that, and I've got to say that I have never felt like a savior or one of the chosen. Everything in my background and training resists that.

But maybe there's another explanation. Maybe the power to overcome and persevere is within all of us. People aren't special because God "chooses" them; they become special because they accept the responsibility. I certainly think I fall into that category. I never felt the urge to thank God after a race in public, as some athletes do. It never bothers me when they do it, but it just isn't my style. But I do believe He gave me the opportunity to succeed, and for me not to have seized it would've been wrong.

For that reason, I don't look upon the responsibilities of being an Olympic champion as a burden or merely something to cash in on. I accept the challenge of being a role model, even if some athletes do not. If you're in the public eye, that's just the way it is. Sometimes it makes you an unfair target and an object of misunderstanding, but fame carries a price. Some athletes may tell the world they don't raise their fans' kids and don't want that responsibility, but that's not what's being asked of them. What's being asked is that they stand as representatives of hope, as symbols, as people to show that with determination and perseverance a person can achieve great things.

One of my favorite post-Olympic memories came when a woman approached me and said, "You would've been a hero and a champion whether you won or not." That really moved me because it bore out what I said about the real battle lying in the struggle. People are happy that I won, of course, but, as with this woman, it was more that they appreciated what I've been through. Maybe it mirrored something in her own life, something that wasn't chronicled on network TV. I think people identify with me because so much of life is struggle and tears and heartache and tragedy. And I'm one example that it can come out right.

I realize that nothing I do with the rest of my life will have the same intensity, will glow quite so brightly, as the 1994 Olympics. But that's okay. It really is. I want to move on, do other things, and, anyway, I have my memories. Yes, many of them will be of those moments in Lillehammer—the race, the medal ceremony, the salute to one Jane, the skate with another Jane. But others are of a more private nature. I'll remember the camaraderie of the sport, the quiet sounds of practice, the sweat, the knowing that Bonnie and Nick were right there on each side of me, feeling what I was feeling, chasing what I was chasing. I'll remember the love and support I received from my family, how much their collective will seemed to pull me along when I was racing. I'll remember the little things. One morning, on an off day during a World Cup competition in Switzerland in 1989, my father and I paid eighteen dollars to take the ski lift to the top of a mountain. I remember it was eighteen dollars because Dad kept saying, "Boy, eighteen dollars is a lot of money for a ride on a lift." We intended to stay for only a couple hours or so to check out the view, but we had lunch and talked and sat around and talked some more and soon it was four o'clock. There was something in the mountain air that brought us together that day, maybe because we felt so close to Jane. You can't replace moments like those, you can only relive them.

Unlike a lot of people right now, I'm not pessimistic about the state of the world. I'm more optimistic, in fact, than I've ever been because of the astonishing number of really good people I've met since Lillehammer. I'm not blind to the world's problems. The absolute tragedy of our times is the millions of kids who grow up in an environment that fosters nothing except drugs and gangs. And when they go to prison, people on the outside sit back and say, "What a loser, what a nothing life."

But it is not their fault. What I saw growing up from my family was love and concern and respect, and those were the ideals I tried to put into my own life. Every single day I'm thankful for that because I have no idea if I would've been able to battle my way out of poverty and a drug-infested environment.

The common theme among people I meet is that so many of them truly want good things for their children. Not material things, like expensive cars and vacation houses, but good things. These are the people I feel I can really help. It's nice to meet the younger kids, the ten- and eleven-year-olds, but sometimes your message is lost because they're in awe of what you accomplished as an athlete. But what I want to tell the young adults and the young parents is that kids need help and support and love, like I had. All those solitary hours I spent training and working toward a goal were really not solitary. My parents, my brothers and sisters, the memory of Jane, and now the love of my wife and child kept me going.

The mission of the future for privileged countries like America is to provide hope and enlightenment to the millions of kids out there who want to live their dreams and achieve their goals, just like I was able to. I challenge all of us to find a way to do that.

ABOUT THE AUTHORS

DAN JANSEN lives in Wisconsin with his wife and baby daughter.

JACK MCCALLUM is a senior writer for *Sports Illustrated* and is the author of *Shaq Attaq!* He lives in Bethlehem, Pennsylvania.